It's a Jungle Out There

GARY RICHMOND

HARVEST HOUSE PUBLISHERS
Eugene, Oregon 97402

IT'S A JUNGLE OUT THERE

Eugene, Oregon 97402

Library of Congress Cataloging-in-Publication Data

Richmond, Gary, 1944–
It's a Jungle Out There / Gary Richmond.
p. cm.
ISBN 1-56507-377-0 (alk. paper)
1. Animals—Religious aspects—Christianity. 2. Richmond, Gary, 1944 .
I. Title.
BT746.R53 1996
242—dc20 95-44476
CIP

Printed in the United States of America.

96 97 98 99 00 01 / BC / 10 9 8 7 6 5 4 3 2

To Hayley Carol and Kendall Thomas

It is a far more wonderful privilege than I had ever imagined . . . being your grandfather. Every smile, loving look, little hug, wave good-bye, and kiss on the cheek makes me so happy and so thankful that God gave you to me. I wanted you to grow up knowing that Papa loves you so very much that he dedicated this book to you.

Contents

Introduction

I do a lot of speaking and have a chance to share these zoo stories with thousands of people, both adults and children. They have been well received, and I hope you enjoy them. I have answered one question recently that has arisen from the hearts of honest children who simply cannot believe so many exciting things could possibly have happened to one man. They ask, "Did these stories really happen?" The answer is *yes,* they really did.

There are, of course, a handful of embellished moments. They are parts of the stories that may have been true. Let me tell you where they are for the sake of integrity.

In the story of Lobo, we never knew for sure how a timber wolf ended up at a dog pound and the meeting with the young couple was fictitious, so I constructed a plausible beginning and end in light of my experience with people who have owned wild animals.

In "The Zoo's Worst Night," the description of the security guard is a combination of two men whom the zookeepers did not like. So this character is half real. The real men experienced enough rejection, and I did not want them to be ridiculed further.

"The Gelada Named Barnaby" is true wherever human observation is concerned. The mountain lion, coyote, and rattlesnake incidents are as close as they can be to what I call possible or even likely fact . . . or fiction. Maybe so, maybe not.

Everything else is true to my best recollection and verified by one or more people who were with me. I hope you have fun reading *It's a Jungle Out There;* I had fun writing it.

Your friend,
Gary Richmond

Chapter One

Ups and Downs

God has designed thousands of ways for members of the animal kingdom to come into existence, but in my estimation the birth of the baby giraffe is of all births the most impressive. See it once and you'll never forget it.

The zoo health center was called at 9:30 A.M. and we were informed that the female Angola giraffe was giving birth. If the veterinarian and I wanted to watch we could. Neither of us had ever witnessed a giraffe birth before, so we headed quickly for the giraffe barn. We parked and walked quietly to a spot where about seven of us were afforded an earthbound view of an elevated event. I sat on a bale of hay next to Jack Badal, a man considered by most of us to be the greatest animal keeper alive. He was a man of few and well-chosen words, and when I sat down, he only nodded and continued to suck the sweetness from the alfalfa stem he had pulled from the hay bale on which we sat.

I noticed the calf's front hooves and head were already visible and dripping with amniotic fluids. I also noticed that the mother was standing up. "When is she going to lie down?" I said to Jack, who still hadn't said anything.

"She won't," he answered.

"But her hindquarters are nearly ten feet off the ground. That calf might get hurt from the fall," I said. Jack just gave me that look that told me I had probably said something that revealed my ignorance.

I wondered why no plans were being made to procure a fireman's net to catch the baby, so I asked. "Listen, Gary," he said. "You can go try to catch the calf if you want, but remember that its mother has enough strength in her hind legs to kick your head off, which is what she'll do if you get anywhere near that calf. Giraffes have killed lions that tried to get their calves."

I was able to sit quietly for a while and observe the calf's journey down the birth canal. Its neck and front legs were fully extended and dangling freely, ten feet above the hard ground on which it was soon to fall. It seemed unbelievable to me that in just a few minutes this newborn was going to be introduced to such trauma. Ten feet! To the hard ground! (It had taken me twelve years to get up the nerve to jump off a high-dive about ten feet high into clear deep water. This giraffe calf was going to top that during its first 30 minutes of visible existence.)

The moment we had anticipated was not a disappointment. The calf, a plucky male, hurled forth, falling ten feet and landing on his back. Within seconds, he rolled to an upright position with his legs tucked under his body. From this position he considered the world for the first time, shaking some of the last vestiges of birthing fluids from his eyes and ears.

The mother giraffe lowered her head long enough to take a quick look. Then she positioned herself so that she was standing directly over her calf. She waited for about a minute and then did the most unreasonable thing. She swung her pendulous leg outward and kicked her baby so that it was sent sprawling head over heels (or hooves, in this case).

I turned to Jack and exclaimed, "Why'd she do that?"

"She wants it to get up, and if it doesn't she'll do it again."

Jack was right—the violent process was repeated again and then again. The struggle to rise was momentous, and as the baby grew tired of trying, the mother would again stimulate its efforts with a hearty kick.

Finally, amidst the cheers of the animal care staff, the calf stood for the first time. Wobbly, for sure, but it stood. Then we were struck silent when she kicked it off its feet again.

Jack's face was the only one not expressing astonishment. "She wants it to remember how it got up," he offered. "That's why she knocked it down. In the wild it would need to get up as soon as possible to follow the herd. The mother needs the herd, too. Lions, hyenas, leopards, and hunting dogs all would enjoy a young giraffe. They'd get it, too, if the mother didn't teach her baby to get up quickly and get with it."

Jack then waved good-bye with his alfalfa stem and returned to his section of the zoo to care for his animals, something he did better than anyone I have ever known.

• • •

I've thought about the birth of that giraffe many times since that spring morning and have seen its parallel in my own life. There have been many times when difficult circumstances have knocked me off my feet. Sooner or later I would get back up . . . only to be knocked down by the next trial. During such times, I would get frustrated because I felt like I wasn't making much progress as a Christian. I'm sure that's a feeling you can identify with as well.

Yet I've come to learn that when a trial comes along, it is God helping me to remember how it was that I got up before. He is gently urging me always to walk with Him—in His shadow under His care.

It's easy for us to view trials as unwelcome intruders in our lives. But they do have a way of prompting us to get up and seek the protection of our heavenly Father. As James reminds us, "Count it all joy, my brethren, when you meet various trials, for you know that the testing of your faith produces steadfastness" (James 1:2-3).

Chapter Two

Chaca, Uh Uh

The phone rang. I looked up at the clock, and it was 12:20 A.M.

My first thought was, *Who died?* After all, why else would anybody call at that time in the morning?

"Hello," I answered. *This better be really good or really bad,* I thought to myself.

"Richmond, how would you like a little adventure in your life?" I recognized the voice of my boss, the zoo's young but very capable veterinarian.

"Sure. What's up?"

"The police just called. They want us to catch a killer ape that's loose in Highland Park. Meet me at the zoo in a few minutes."

As I hung up the phone I found myself wishing he had not said "killer ape." Of course if a killer ape were loose in Highland Park it would need our help. That was a rough neighborhood.

I pushed my car to its limits and the freeway lights and

signs charged past me like an onslaught of wooden soldiers. They briefly appeared in my rearview mirror and quickly faded from view. As I drove, I took inventory of what we might need to capture the killer ape: tranquilizer gun, nets, ropes, and assorted drugs. My damp palms gripped the steering wheel, and I wondered if my boss would notice if I didn't show up. I was probably the only person he had called, so I concluded he might.

I skidded around the freeway offramp and entered the zoo's immense parking lot. Waiting at the entrance to the zoo was a black and white police car, its red and yellow lights pulsating with anticipation. Two officers were sitting in the front seat.

"Your boss is already at the health center. He wanted us to bring you up." I jumped in the back of the police car and we screamed past the security guard who was manning the gate.

"Killer ape, huh?" I asked.

"Tore up his master real good. Went after one of our officers too. That ape is one mean son of a gun." (The officer didn't exactly say "son of a gun.") "One of our guys discharged his revolver at it, but he missed. We'll get the sucker, though."

By the time we pulled up to the zoo health center, Dr. Bill Hulsizer had already gathered everything we would need. We threw it in the trunk and jumped into the back seat. The car lurched forward, and in no time we were on the freeway with the siren howling. We passed several cars, all of which looked as though they were standing still. I glanced at the speedometer and noticed that we were going 90 miles an hour.

I turned to Bill and asked, "So what do you think we're up against?"

He was the scientific type and would not speculate. He shrugged his shoulders and said, "We'll see."

I have always suffered from an overactive imagination, and it wouldn't have surprised me if King Kong himself stepped on the police car when we got there. We flew down the offramp and wove our way deep into a residential area. As we drew closer to our destination, the officers were stopped by a crusty sergeant who pointed into the night and said, "They're waitin' for you at the command post."

"Command post," I said with a tinge of sarcasm in my voice. "What did you get us into, Doctor?"

"We'll see," he said with a wry smile. Boy, sometimes those scientific types can really make you mad.

At the command post it looked as though we had entered a war zone. There were police cars everywhere. All of them had their lights flashing on and off, and many people from the neighborhood were clustered in small groups, discussing the crisis. We arrived at the command post, and an officer with plenty of authority called for a mass meeting. Officers began showing up from everywhere. I'm sure there were more than 50. We were brought to the center of the group and the officer with all the authority said, "Men, this is Dr. Bill Hulsizer and his assistant Gary Richmond. These guys are experts from the zoo. They're going to help us track down the ape." Then he turned to us and said, "You guys are in charge. What do you want us to do?"

Bill and I looked at each other, and I think we both wanted to laugh. Bill was the shy type. He was a very competent veterinarian, but there was no way he was going to order around the policemen that surrounded us. I didn't want to usurp his authority so I waited for him to make the first move. He put his arm on my shoulder and said, "Gary is the capture expert. Let's let him take charge."

"Take it," said the man with the biggest badge. So I did.

"Is there anybody here who has seen the animal we are after?" I probed.

A young officer stepped forward and said, "I did, sir."

"Can you describe him for us?"

"The lighting wasn't too good. He was big, though. I discharged my revolver at him, but I believe I missed. Scared the heck out of me." (The officer didn't exactly say "heck.")

"Is the owner around here or are there any neighbors who have seen the animal? They might be able to help us know what we are after."

The owner's father was brought to us, and as it turned out, he was the man who had been attacked. Most of his upper body was bandaged, including his face. The owner was in jail on several counts, all having to do with possessing or selling narcotics. Apparently he had developed a drug habit in Vietnam and brought it home with him. But that's not all he brought home. He also brought along a young pet that grew up into a large and dangerous animal.

I asked the man if he had a photograph of his son's pet. He said he did and reached for his wallet. As he handed me the picture, he explained how he had gotten his injuries. Because the son was in jail, the responsibility of feeding the creature went to the father. The creature only liked the son, and attempting to get food into the cage each day was an act of courage. This was the night the father lost the battle. Blood was seeping through his gauze bandages, and I could just feel the tension building among the officers.

I studied the photograph and was somewhat relieved to discover that the "killer ape" was really just a large monkey. He was a stump-tailed macaque—a very large specimen with two-inch canines.

I addressed the father once more. "Is there anything the monkey likes?" I was thinking of a favorite food item and was unprepared for the man's answer.

He was a Mexican-American gentleman and said with great enthusiasm, "Chaca likes it when you say, 'Chaca, uh uh.' I don't know why, but it calms him down." I thanked the man for his help and turned to the assembly of policemen.

"Officers, I have very good news for you. We are not after a killer ape, but a very large monkey named Chaca.

Chaca is not the kind of animal that you would need to shoot, and frankly, I will not help you look for him if I have to worry about getting shot. If it would make you feel better, carry your nightsticks with you. The owner's father has just told me that the monkey likes it when you say, 'Chaca, uh uh,' so I suggest that as you go through the neighborhood you repeat that phrase over and over. We will wait here until he is sighted; then we will take over. He is most likely scared to death after being shot at and is simply hiding."

As the officers spread out, Dr. Hulsizer leaned over to me and said, "Gary, it's not going to do any good for them to be saying, 'Chaca, uh uh.'"

"It will too. It will keep them calm. If they think they're helping their own cause, they might not shoot each other." Then Bill and I got the giggles as Los Angeles's finest went from house to house and from garage to garage saying, "Chaca, uh uh."

A police helicopter thundered overhead and turned on its blinding searchlight. Backyards were bathed in light, and although it was 2:00 A.M., we had the passing sensation of walking about in broad daylight. Walkie-talkies crackled and squeaked as policemen checked in to report that they had not sighted Chaca.

Eventually the helicopter search was called off, and we again heard the masculine chant, "Chaca, uh uh . . . Chaca, uh uh." It was as if we were hearing a soundtrack from an old jungle movie and it would have fit the moment perfectly if someone had said, "The natives are getting restless."

At 2:45 A.M., an officer came running up to us and announced that his partner had Chaca cornered in a garage. We grabbed our equipment and hurried to the site. Most of the policemen were already there. They parted to let us through so that we could enter the side door of the garage. When we got inside, we saw Chaca huddled under a small fishing boat that was sitting snugly on its boat trailer. Chaca was protecting his face from the bright beam of light that came from the sergeant's blue-steel flashlight. Chaca's body language was screaming, "Don't shoot! Please don't shoot!"

His capture was not in the least dramatic. We laid a net over his trembling body and he fell over. I believe he was very close to fainting. We transferred Chaca to a travel cage and took him back to the zoo. He was kept there for 30 days in quarantine to determine whether or not he was carrying any transmissible diseases. He was then moved to another facility and we never saw him again.

It was after 4:00 A.M. when I crawled back into bed. Our time in Highland Park had been a great adventure—an adventure with a happy, injury-free conclusion. It was clearly one of the more memorable experiences of my life.

As I look back on that incident, I cannot recall any deliberate thought concerning God during the whole night. But I know that He was there, caring, protecting. God never sleeps or slumbers; He watches over us both night and day.

One of the most comforting thoughts that I have ever entertained comes from a poem by Ruth Harms Calkins. I've excerpted these words from her classic book of poems, *Tell Me Again Lord, I Forget.*

> Loving me as you do,
> You understand so well,
> That when I want you least
> I need you most.[1]

You see, even when we are not thinking of God, He is thinking of us. He is always present with us. Though we may not be aware of it, He is very much involved in every moment of our lives.

If you would like to see affirmation of that truth, then take a few moments now to read the book of Esther. It's the only book in the Bible that never mentions God in any way. Nothing supernatural is recorded. But from the first page to the last, God is there, developing the character of a beautiful woman and protecting His people.

Indeed, God is the same yesterday, today, and forever (Hebrews 13:8). The same God who watched over Esther is watching over us this very moment. What a comforting assurance!

---

1. From *Tell Me Again, Lord, I Forget* by Ruth Harms Calkin. Published by Tyndale House Publishers, Inc., © 1986. Used by permission.

Chapter Three

Be Careful—You Might Let Out a Bear

I'll never forget the feelings I experienced when two shiny new keys were pressed firmly into my trembling hands. They weren't just any keys. These keys gave me access to all the cages at the Los Angeles Zoo. The supervisor admonished me solemnly concerning the use and care of these keys.

"Richmond," he said, "these keys will let you in to care for millions of dollars worth of animals. Some of them could never be replaced, but you could be, if you catch my drift. Some of the animals would hurt themselves if they got out, and more significantly, they might hurt and even kill somebody. You wouldn't want that on your conscience.

"And, Richmond, don't lose the keys. The big boys in administration don't take it too well if you lose the keys. It works out best if they don't hear your name much until you pass probation six months from now."

The longer we talked, the heavier the keys became. I discovered that most of the veterans (five years or more of service) had let out animals. And if I stayed at the zoo, sooner or later that would happen to me. Somehow my job security was tied to how I cared for these keys, and they seemed heavier still.

The supervisor gave me several tips on key care, use, and safety, and emphasized the value of getting into a routine. "Consistency is your best safeguard," he said. "Do your routine the same way at every exhibit. Develop a good habit and don't vary your routine."

I took him seriously and performed flawlessly for four months. I received sterling evaluations for my safety habits—but then one day I made a mistake.

I wouldn't be able to tell you why my routine varied, but somehow it did, and with the most dangerous animal at the zoo. Ivan was a polar bear who weighed well over 900 pounds and had killed two prospective mates. He hated people and never missed an opportunity to attempt to grab them as they passed by his cage. Many of us had experienced nightmares featuring Ivan. And one of the concerns most discussed among the keepers was the horrifying question, "What if Ivan got out?"

For more than 100 consecutive workdays I had cared for this nightmare, never coming close to making a mistake. Then one day I let him out of his night quarters into the sparkling morning sunshine by pulling a lever that lifted a 500-pound steel guillotine door. No sooner had he passed under it than I realized that the steel door that had given me access to the outside exhibit (where Ivan was now) was still wide open. At any minute he might be walking down the hall and around the corner. My inclination was to run. Not wanting to be fired, however, I chose to stay.

I lifted the guillotine door again, and to my relief, Ivan was in view. He was a creature of routine, and he always spent the first hour of his morning pacing. His pattern was L-shaped. He would walk from the door five steps straight out and then turn right for three steps. He would then rock back and forth and come back to the guillotine door, which he would bump with his head. He would repeat that cycle for one hour and then rest.

I timed Ivan's pacing cycle and determined that I had 17 seconds to run down the hallway and shut the open door. I staked my life on his consistency. He didn't seem to notice the wide-open door, which was unusual. Animals tend to notice any changes in their environment.

I decided that when Ivan made his next turn, I would run down the L-shaped concrete hallway, hoping upon hope that I would not see Ivan.

When he turned, I ran. With every step my knees weakened. My heart pounded so hard I felt sure it would burst from fear. I made the corner and faced the critical moment. Ivan was still out of sight; I lunged for the door handle. As I reached for the handle I looked to the right. There was the bear, eight feet away. Our eyes met. His were cold and unfeeling and I'm sure mine expressed all the terror that filled the moment. I pulled the huge steel door with all my strength. It clanged shut and the clasp was secured. My knees buckled and I fell to the floor racked by the effect of too much adrenaline. I looked up, and Ivan was staring at me through the viewing window of the hallway door.

I had almost let out a bear—the worst bear at the zoo. All because I did not adhere to a simple habit I had followed to keep animals from escaping their cages.

• • •

All of us have daily habits we follow in an effort to keep our lives free of problems. For example, we brush our teeth to prevent tooth decay. We change the oil in our cars to keep the engine running smoothly. And in the Christian life, there are certain disciplines that can help us stand firm in our faith. It is these disciplines, or habits, that enable us to grow mature.

Perhaps you're wondering: What do we mean by disciplines? Let's consider a few.

One of the most important and most often neglected is *regular prayer,* talking with God. Another is good, old-fashioned *perseverance.* That is, sticking with the task until it's done—having a singleminded focus on the job at hand. Yet another is *learning to be obedient,* or getting in the habit of doing what is right. Writer Eugene Peterson extols the value of this discipline in his book aptly titled *A Long Obedience in the Same Direction.* Then there is the habit of *telling the truth,* which is a hallmark of consistency and trustworthiness. We're likely to get caught when we don't tell the truth, as Mark Twain reminds us when he says, "If you tell the truth, you don't have to remember anything."

Much like the habits I developed at the zoo were intended to protect both the animals and the visitors, the habits you cultivate in your Christian life can protect you. Consider these words from Hebrews 5:14: "Solid food is for the mature, who because of practice have their senses trained to discern good and evil."

Consistent living produces its own protection. Seek it. Cherish it. It may keep you from letting out a bear.

Chapter Four

An Otter Named Girl

It couldn't have been more than three days into my zoo career that I was warned by the senior animal keeper not to make pets of any of the animals under my care.

"There are good reasons for this, Gary," he said. "First, I want you to remember that it's the tame ones that get you. You tame them and, sure, everything goes along fine for six months or so, and then, bang, your animal has a bad day. Now that's just fine if you're talking white rat or poodle, but if we're talking leopard, wolf, chimp, or ostrich, that's a different story. When they have a bad day, you have a bad day. I'm talking losing fingers and eyes, breaking bones, and even losing your life. Are you following me, Gary?"

I knew enough to nod yes.

"There are some other things you should think about. When you tame an animal and turn it into a pet, you begin to feel like it belongs to you. It doesn't. It belongs to the zoo. It will always belong to the zoo, so don't start thinking any different. You won't always be working in this section. If you've turned a bunch of these animals into pets and the bosses decide to transfer you to teach you more or use your gifts better, then you'll feel like they're trying to punish you. You'll feel like they're taking your pets away from you, but that won't be the case at all.

"One more thing: It's hard on the animals when they get attached to you and you get transferred or quit the zoo. Animals do better when they don't have to make too many adjustments. They are healthier and they get along with their own kind better. That means they'll have more babies. We want them to have lots and lots of babies, so don't go making any of the animals on your string into pets."

All that made good sense to me, and most of the animals in the aquatics section didn't make good pets anyway. Ivan the polar bear was a killer and didn't like people at all. The alligators were certainly too dangerous and could never be trusted. The male elephant seal chased me out of his exhibit every time I cleaned it. I think he thought his females liked me too much, and he was very jealous. They did like me because I fed them 25 pounds of fish every day. Mr. and Mrs. Beaver were very unfriendly and even turned their backs to me whenever I was around.

There were a few animals that would have been fun to tame and one group that was already tame but not trained. The California sea lions were very tame, and though we were never allowed to pet them, we could walk among them without any fear of being attacked. At the time, there were no large bulls (males), and all the females were sweethearts. This was good for me because there wasn't any place we could put them when we cleaned their exhibit. We had to be in the exhibit with them.

Following the no-pet rule was easy most of the time, but eventually I did wish I could have made friends with the Canadian river otters. Otters were just the kind of animal that you would want to have as a pet. They have friendly faces and are active, curious, and playful. Their fur is prized for its softness and beauty.

There was one female otter that was especially friendly. She would often stand at the gate and watch me preparing their food or cleaning their quarters. She really looked as though she would like to be friends, but I kept my resolve and willed to believe that my senior keeper was right about leaving wild animals wild.

One day while I was cleaning the otters' night quarters, the chief keeper (my boss's boss) paid me a visit. He was a large man of American Indian descent. He was kind and soft-spoken. As a group, the keepers respected his many years of experience with animals.

He said, "Richmond, are any of our otters tame?"

"One seems a little friendly, but none of them are tame," I answered.

"You know anything about training or taming animals?"

"I've never done anything with zoo animals, but I have a real obedient collie at home."

"How would you like to take a shot at taming one of your otters, the friendly one? Seems as though our public-relations people promised some Hollywood producer that we'd be able to bring a tame otter to a movie premiere in Hollywood two months from now. The boys down at administration said that would be fine, and I think we're stuck to try. They are your animals, so you get first shot, but if you want me to, I could get a relief keeper to do it. You don't have to teach it any tricks. All you need to do is get to the point where the otter won't bite anyone who tries to pet it. That may turn out to be a tall order, and I wouldn't blame you if you didn't want to try."

I have made a profession of rushing in where angels never go, so I said yes before thinking through the implications of my decision. We shook hands. My father had taught me that a handshake was a solemn contract, so I was bound to do everything in my power to deliver a tame otter in 60 days. And remember, when you're young, 60 days seems like an eternity. From my perspective I had all the time in the world to tame an otter. But I soon came to realize that otters knew nothing of handshakes and deadlines.

Fred told me I could take as much time as I needed to work on taming the otter, even if it meant letting other work slide. Aquatics was a large section, so my one worry was having enough time to finish my daily work and tame the otter too.

The next morning I asked some of the guys who had been at the zoo a long time if they could give me some tips on taming an otter. Every one of them was helpful, and I went away with more ideas than I could try. I did settle on a plan that seemed to me to be the most likely to work.

I started by cutting back on the otter food so that all of them would be a little hungry all of the time. They were all overweight, so that was not cruel; in fact, it would be good for them. When I was sure that they were hungry, I would bring their favorite food, smelt, a small sardinelike fish, and throw it to them a piece at a time. One of the otters would likely prove to be less afraid and easier to tame, and I would isolate that one and work with it.

Two days passed and I was fairly sure that all the otters were hungry. I stepped into the exhibit and sat down where they could clearly see me from the large pool where they spent most of their day. All of them looked with interest while I let them get used to my presence. I took some small pieces of fish and threw the pieces near where the otters were floating. Otters are curious animals, and they all swam to check out what had been thrown to them. They were all hungry and noisily ate the fish. Then they stared at me to see if I was going to throw more. I did, and they enthusiastically pursued the pieces of fish by diving underwater with their usual fluid grace. Like seals and sea lions, otters are a little clumsy on land but their movements look magical in water. One of the otters didn't eat its fish right away but swam with it. It was almost a ritual, a celebration or game. When the otters swam it was more than swimming; it was ballet. Their turns and rolls were a visual symphony.

I recognized the otter playing with the fish. It was the friendly female. I gently said hello and asked her if she was still hungry. She stared at me. It was easy to see that she was eager for more, so I threw her another piece. She wolfed it down, and her bright eyes stared longingly at the can of smelt. She looked into my eyes to see what I would do. I decided to wait and see if she would come closer. She did not. But she had come to land. I threw another piece of smelt halfway between us and waited to see what she would do. She stared at it and then took one cautious step closer to the fish. I could tell she was nervous. As it turned out, her fear was stronger than her hunger. She looked at me to see if I was going to throw any more fish, and I waited to see if she was going to get the piece I had already thrown. She didn't. She returned to the water, looking over her shoulder now and then to see if she was going to get any more fish from me. I decided that I didn't want to satisfy their smelt desires any more than I had and hoped that I would be able to draw them closer to me later.

The next day I was no more successful. That's when I first began to wonder if I had bitten off more than I could chew. Otters are as independent as cats. It was evident that they could resist hunger. I began sitting closer to the water, hoping that they would feel more secure in the water and venture closer to me to get their fishy snacks. This plan worked well and soon three otters were swimming within five feet of me to receive their portion of fish. I could feel my heart beat with excitement; for the first time I could see progress. They were accepting my presence in their territory and even looking forward to it.

After about two weeks they drew to within a foot of my hand but were still cautious when they ventured near. I could see, as the days passed, their eyes change from fear to mild trust.

One afternoon I entered the exhibit and sat next to the pool. To my astonishment the friendly female swam swiftly toward me, launched out of the water, and stood patiently with happy eyes, waiting for her favorite treat. She startled me with her boldness, and I jumped backward slightly. She held her ground waiting to be fed. I decided to go for it and held out a whole smelt. She was trembling with excitement, and my heart was thumping rapidly as I reached out to her. The closer I extended the fish the more I questioned the wisdom of what I was doing. Otters could deliver a nasty bite, and, though she was not showing any signs of aggression, I was well aware that she might snap at the fish and bite my hand. I resolved to take that chance.

When the fish was two inches from her face, she leaned toward it so delicately, so gently, so carefully that it was clear she felt she was safe. Her mouth opened slowly and shut softly on the smelt. I let go and carefully withdrew my hand. She took hold of the fish and ate it like an ice cream cone. It was a wonderful moment. It was a magical moment. The sounds of the zoo visitors, monkeys hooting in the background, and bird song all seemed to fade and give way to the wonder of this moment that I had wished for for days. It was as if the world stood still so that I might be presented, at heaven's hand, the gift of a lifelong memory.

I watched with wonder as she savored her delicacy. She was cute up close and she showed no fear. The first step had been taken with five weeks to go. She ate three more fish, always being careful not to touch my hand with her razor-sharp teeth. She dove back into the pool and the spell was broken, but the joy of finally having good news to report overwhelmed me. To the surprise of the zoo visitors, I shouted, "Yahoo!" and threw the rest of the smelt to the startled otters.

I ran to the chief keeper's office and said, "She finally took food out of my hand. It was great! She ate it right in front of me as if I weren't even there. She ate four fish not two feet away from me and showed no signs of fear at all!"

"You're halfway home, Gary. I knew you could do it. Your next step is to get her to crawl on your lap. Then see if she will let you touch her. After that it gets tougher. If she lets you pick her up you're almost finished. If you get that far, I'll tell you what to do after that. Good luck, man. Stay with it."

Our progress was swift now that the fear barrier was down. Her trust in me grew daily. It was four days until she stayed on my lap. I conditioned her to human contact by placing some fish on the other side of my legs from her. At first she walked around, but then she reached the point where she was comfortable just climbing over me to get to the smelt.

I knew that we had to move on to the next level and decided to dangle a fish in front of my face. She jumped on my lap, placed her front feet on my chest, and took the fish. She surprised me by staying on my lap to eat it. I fed her several fish, one at a time, and she ate them all in a polite and ladylike manner.

Otters, like dolphins, have naturally happy faces, and when they look into your eyes you feel loved. We were bonding, and I could feel a strong attachment building. I knew I was breaking a rule because she really did feel like my otter. I felt angry at the thought that I might be transferred away from her.

Another thought that crossed my mind was that she didn't have a name. Now that we were friends, I felt like I should call her something. I wanted it to be a ladylike name, something Canadian. I thought and thought, but nothing came. I decided that sooner or later a good name would come to me, but until then I settled for calling her "Girl." After a week Girl seemed like her name, and I was never able to think of anything that fit her better. So Girl stuck. It wasn't all that original, but it was accurate.

The day after she stood on my lap she surprised me again. After eating a bunch of smelt, she stayed on my lap to groom. She licked her paws clean; cleaned, combed, and oiled her hair; and then stretched out and went to sleep. I couldn't believe my eyes. If this wasn't trust, nothing was.

She slept with her head in her paws for awhile and then rolled over on her back. I loved the contact and this breakthrough in our relationship, but my legs began to go to sleep and I wanted to shift for comfort's sake. It dawned on me that this might be the perfect time to see if I could pet her. I carefully laid my hand against her shoulder and slowly drew it down her back. She stirred, looked at my hand, stood up, and looked at me as if to say, "Do you want me to move?" Then she yawned and stretched and walked to the pool. I wasn't sure whether or not we had crossed the next barrier, so I chose not to report it to the chief keeper, especially if I couldn't demonstrate it.

The next day I tried to pet Girl while she was awake, and she stretched out to enjoy it. My report was made, but with only two weeks to go I was anything but sure she would be ready for the premiere. The next day she allowed me to pet her more vigorously, and for the first time she played. She mouthed my hand, only gently. She pretended to bite and growled, but it was clearly a game. We both enjoyed it for several minutes.

You might wonder what the other otters were doing all these weeks. They had come to the point where they would eat from my hand, but that was it. They would watch Girl and me and our new games with interest, but they stayed to themselves for the most part. On a couple of occasions they stood and leaned against my leg to beg for food, but if I sat down they kept their distance.

One day while Girl and I were playing, a lady asked if Girl would let me pick her up. I told her I hadn't tried. She asked if I would know when Girl was ready, and I had to admit that I wasn't sure. She said simply, "Well, why don't you try?" I shrugged my shoulders and said, "Why not?"

Girl was leaning against my chest. I scratched her back vigorously. I kept scratching her back and then supported her with the palm of one hand. Surprisingly, she climbed on my shoulders and held on as I rose to full stature. She didn't seem panicked, and the lady zoo visitor clapped and said, "Bravo!"

Not wanting to press my luck, I sat down again so that Girl wouldn't panic and jump. The last thing I wanted was for her to hurt herself. We had come so far and, with only ten days to go, I couldn't have any setbacks. Still I had held her on my shoulder, and she had seemed to enjoy the improved view of her exhibit.

I reported to Fred that Girl was letting me hold her now, and he was very pleased. He said that he thought we just might make it. "Now she still has a way to go," he said. "We have to find out if you're the only one she will trust. We need to condition her to riding in a car. She might like men but not women. She may not like perfumes or shaving lotions. We need to see how she does when you dress differently. What you need to do is start treating her like she's going to the premiere of *Ring of Bright Water.* You have to think what she might face and try it on her; then we can make the decision whether or not she's ready to go."

The next day I brought Dale Thompson into the exhibit with me, and Girl was as tame for him as she was for me. Dale was excellent with animals and was the perfect choice for working with her also. Best of all, it was fun to share this adventure with my best friend. We tried on several different shaving lotions and colognes. Although she would sniff at us, she still knew who we were and delighted in our company. We invited several ladies from the children's zoo, and Girl was as enchanted to play with them as they were with her. We drove her around the zoo in my car, and she stayed on my shoulder. We got out several places, and she seemed satisfied to stay in my arms and let other keepers pet her. With five days to go, it seemed as though she was ready. But the final decision was in the hands of the chief keeper, Fred Rose. We invited him to go the course with us, and Girl was a perfect lady. She passed her tests with flying colors. He looked at me and said, "Good job. She seems to be ready."

We were going to a Hollywood premiere, and Girl was going to steal the show. I was just sure of it!

The next four days were dress rehearsals for the real thing. Each day I was more confident that everything was as fine as could be. I was so proud of Girl. She had become more like a dog than an otter, running up to greet me every time I came to the exhibit. She made me look good, and all of this was going to look good at evaluation time, which was coming up soon.

The 60 days had zoomed by. The day of the premiere finally dawned, and I awoke with a stomach full of butterflies and a bad case of the "what ifs." What if I had forgotten to think of something that would shake Girl up? Surely no movie stars would bring their dogs to the premiere, would they? That would shake her up. No, they wouldn't do that. What if some chauffeur honked his limousine horn and frightened her? That could happen, I thought, but I could probably calm her down again. Stop worrying, I thought. Everything will be fine. It's going to be a super night.

I got to work and Girl was as perky and affectionate as usual. The chief keeper let me know that Channel 7 News was going to film inside the otter exhibit, which was great. Girl was used to being photographed and that would be a nice practice run for the premiere. Piece of cake.

"What time?" I asked.

"About three o'clock, they said. But I think it would be a good idea if you hung out by the otters from about two o'clock on, in case we need you."

"Sure, Fred, I'll be there if you need me."

"You did a good job, Gary. Everybody will remember this for a long time."

Fred didn't know how prophetic he was. I didn't know how quickly the tide could turn, but I would find out.

At 2:30 I saw Fred walking swiftly toward the otter exhibit. He was out of breath and looked a little worried.

"What's up, Fred?" I asked.

"How do you think Girl will act around another kind of animal?" he asked a little out of breath.

"I don't know. I never thought to try," I answered.

"Well, we're sure going to find out real soon. One of the big wheels over at the network thought it would be nice to have a chimpanzee at the news conference with the otter. The president of the zoo association said sure, no problem. I told them I wasn't too sure that this was the best day to bring a chimp over, but they said the network was doing us a big favor with the publicity, so let's just give them what they ask for."

I had a sick feeling that this was not going to work and prepared myself for the worst. Girl was getting a pop quiz just before her final exam, and in my heart I knew she would not be up to it.

Important people began to arrive with people whose job it is to make important people feel important. Important questions were asked and answered. Questions like, "How have you been, darling? I haven't seen you since the Stewarts' party, or was it the benefit?" "You look marvelous, darling. How is my hair and makeup?" "I've just been so pushed all day. Anyway, darling, it's really so sweet of you to come. . . ."

I stood over to the side, holding Girl, who wanted to play hostess to her visitors, but I wanted to be holding her when the chimp came through the gate. One of the celebrities noticed us and smiled. He came over and asked if he could pet Girl. I said sure. He commented on how soft her fur was and was really quite taken by her friendly charm. He returned to the group of celebrities and ended up being the only one to enjoy the wonder of this terrific otter.

The chimp arrived. Girl noticed it in an instant and leapt from my arms and headed for her pool. She entered the pool but jumped up on the edge to see if the new hairy invader meant any harm. She stared like a bird dog at point at the chimp, and then slowly, with extravagant caution, she walked between the legs of the visitors to get a better look at the chimp. The chimp was holding hands with a zoo attendant and looked like a hairy toddler out for a walk with its mother.

When the chimp noticed Girl, it screamed and took a protective swipe at her. That was all Girl needed to know that something dangerous, something evil, had entered her world. There was no love in her eyes. That light had gone out. I had seen this look 60 days before. It represented fear and caution, and I even felt a touch of betrayal. She smelled the now-strong scent of the chimp and lifted her nose to make a memory of this invasion. When I tried to pick her up, she growled at me but didn't bite. I knew enough not to push her and just let her run around between people's legs and keep an eye on the chimp.

The director looked unhappy with me and said, "I was told this animal was tame."

"Yes, sir, she is, with everyone but chimpanzees. She's never seen one before, and as it turns out she doesn't like them."

He just scowled at Girl and walked away. The filming started, and I could do nothing but apologize for her lack of hospitality. *Ring of Bright Water* was a movie about an otter, and it seemed silly to me to be bringing a chimp in at this moment to satisfy a man who didn't know a thing about animals. But still, as I look back, the public probably ate up all the chimp footage even more than they would have the otter. At the time I felt that the best animal at the zoo was being upstaged. Tame chimps, as cute as this one was, are a dime a dozen; tame otters a rare delight. Sixty days of hope and hard work were trashed and trampled under that chimp's feet.

When everyone left the otter exhibit, I stayed behind to calm Girl, but she would not be comforted. The chimp had left its scent behind, and all Girl could do was look for the animal whose scent seemed to be everywhere. She would not let me hold her, but she didn't mind being petted while she looked unsuccessfully for the hairy, dark intruder. I started to believe we were in trouble when she wouldn't eat any fish.

At five o'clock, she still would not let me pick her up. Our bond was temporarily broken. We needed to leave for Hollywood in 15 minutes. My senior keeper joined me in the back of her exhibit and asked if he could help me get her leash on. I held her while he tried to slip the chain over her neck. She gave me a dirty look and then attacked the senior keeper viciously. I pulled her back, thinking I would be bitten also, but she just wiggled out my grasp and ran back into the exhibit to look for the chimp.

"The chimp really shook her up, Al. She wouldn't have done that to you if they hadn't brought the chimp around," I said.

"I suspect you're right, Gary. But she's not going to let you hold her anymore today, and the best we can do is bring them a live otter in a cage. We can't trust her not to bite someone while she's in this mood."

His arm was all the proof we needed. Down deep I knew he was right. Al got a cage and a net, and Girl was captured. She hated the cage. She paced back and forth during the whole premiere that night. Not only was she a delight; several people were feeling sorry for her.

That night, when we returned her to the zoo, Girl was exhausted. She ran out of the small cage and joined her friends, who were sleeping. They lifted their heads long enough to greet her and then lay back down. Girl laid her head on the back of a male. Our eyes met for several seconds. She looked kind again, though very tired. I wondered, if she could talk, would she ask me what the last 60 days had been all about? I wondered what an otter thought about when its world is turned upside down after so many days of gentle kindness.

My senior keeper had been right, and his wisdom echoed in my mind. Don't turn your animals into pets.

I whispered, "Good night, Girl. Sorry." Then I went home a sadder but wiser young man. Wiser because I had learned some lessons the hard way—lessons I would never forget. First, I learned again that you can do all the right things, and things can still go wrong. I learned that even when stories have sad endings, they can have happy middles and good beginnings. You see, I will forever treasure my magical moments with Girl and remember the feel of her silken fur on my cheek and the smell of sweet sushi on her breath. I will remember the loving looks and the snuggling. I will remember her greetings and the trust that she gave as a gift, given only one time and only to me.

I gave her a gift, too. I let her slowly learn to be an otter again, weaning her gently from the constant care and favor that she had received at my hand. She learned again to be an otter. Should I see Girl in heaven, we will again be friends as before, but for now it will be easier for me to let wild animals be wild as God meant them to be.

Taming Girl in 60 days seemed at the time a hard test, a difficult assignment. That happened 20 years ago. Since that time I have seen many greater accomplishments. I have seen tame lions and jaguars, tamed by men and women braver and more skilled than I. I played with those animals at another zoo. I enjoy the friendship of Jack Badal, whom I believe to be the greatest animal man alive today and one of the world's great animal trainers. Jack has the distinction of being the only man to have trained a gorilla to perform a full act as alertly as a chimpanzee. I have played with tamed wolves, coyotes, foxes, orangutans, snow leopards, pythons, boa constrictors, and animals whose names you have probably never heard before.

As wonderful as my days with Girl were, they now seem surprisingly common. I was intrigued to find an assessment of my work in the book of James: "All kinds of animals, birds, reptiles and creatures of the sea are being tamed and have been tamed by man" (James 3:7). The next verse says, "But no man can tame the tongue. It is a restless evil, full of deadly poison." God would applaud a tame tongue, but no man will ever accomplish that under his own power. It simply takes more time and more strength of character than any of us can muster under our own steam.

That's the bad news, but there is good news to report too. God has both the power and the will to tame our tongues; He just requires that we request His services. So it matters little the evil or wickedness our tongue is enacting—God can bring it under control so that we stop hurting people. If we are lying, He will help us to have the courage to tell the truth. If we just can't seem to stop gossiping, God alone will help. If we have become used to saying filthy and offensive words, He will help us stop it. If we complain too much, He will help us to see all the reasons to be glad. God can change our tongue overnight, but He waits for us to be willing.

God has done a lot of remodeling in my mouth, and the taste of poison is faint now but still capable of causing even those I love most terrible pain. So I am still asking for help. Why not join me and show the world a real rare animal, a tame tongue? If you are like me, looking for good incentives to clean up your act, then consider these verses that describe the power of a healthy tongue:

> Do not let any unwholesome talk come out of your mouths, but only what is helpful for building others up according to their needs, that it may benefit those who listen (Ephesians 4:29 NIV).

> A word fitly spoken is like apples of gold in a setting of silver (Proverbs 25:11).

Chapter Five

Nowhere to Go

If you think a South American jaguar is impressive when she bares her teeth and snarls from the confines of her cage, you should see her just after she has escaped. It's an experience that will continue to haunt you for weeks to come.

I was sitting at my desk one afternoon updating the lowland gorilla's polio immunization records when the head of the zoo security force called.

"We've got ourselves an emergency," he blurted. "A big cat got out of her cage and attacked a keeper. We need you and your boss right now!"

I ran for the lab where Dr. Bernstein was checking test results with our lab technician.

"We've got a hot one, Doc. Big cat's loose in the South American section. Probably a jaguar. Keeper's been hurt."

He nodded and we grabbed our emergency gear and headed for the truck. You know that these things will happen occasionally but you never feel quite prepared when they do. We made speculation on who might have been hurt and hoped it was not too serious. A senior keeper ran to meet us as soon as the truck screeched to a halt in back of the jaguar exhibit. He filled us in while we got our equipment together.

"Jaguar's loose, Doc. We'll need her tranquilized. She jumped Whittle. Looks like he'll be okay but his arm's broken. When the jag jumped him, he got his arm in her mouth. Security is taking him to the hospital now."

"Where's the public?" I inquired. It was 4:15 on a Monday afternoon. There wouldn't be a crowd, but there would be a few people wandering around.

"Yeah, we thought of that too. We rounded them up and locked them in the restrooms till we get the cat."

"Good idea."

"Let's go get her before she does any more damage," said the doctor.

The jaguar had been contained in a most original and primitive way. Several animal keepers had been called to the scene and were directed to bring trash can lids and rakes. They surrounded the animal, then yelled and beat the trash can lids whenever she attempted to leave the area. It looked like a scene more suited to India at the turn of the century than Los Angeles in the early seventies.

We began to prepare the tranquilizer dart, carefully measuring the proper dose necessary to bring down the jaguar. The dangers of shooting her with the dart were as follows: 1) Big cats don't fall asleep right away. With the proper dosage, the drop time would be about five minutes. 2) A high percentage of the darts misfire and don't inject anything but fatty tissue. You have to wait quite a while before you can shoot again because the animal may have received a full dose that is seeping out of a deep layer of fat. 3) Some animals get very angry when you shoot them with a dart because it has a large-gauge needle that causes a fair amount of pain.

Now it stands to reason that all of these factors are much more significant when the animal is outside the cage. Upon being provoked she would be inclined to attack someone, most likely the person who had shot her with the rifle. That would be me. As I got ready, my mouth was dry, my heart was pounding, and I was shaking so hard that I wished someone would help adjust my vertical hold. I raised the gun to my shoulder and began to zero in on the most muscular portion of the jaguar's hindquarters. She looked at me and I stopped breathing for a second. I would pull the trigger when she looked away.

The silence was shattered by the arrival of our assistant director, Dr. Nathan Gale.

"Don't shoot!" he yelled with firm authority.

I lowered the gun and he joined us for a brief conference.

"Listen, guys, she just wants back in her cage. If we shoot her and the dart misfires she might run for the hills. If she gets loose in Griffith Park it might take a week to find her. The police would order her shot and we don't want that. Let's just apply gentle pressure and guide her back to her cage. When she sees the open door, she'll run in."

I repeated an axiom to myself: *The boss may not always be right, but the boss is always the boss.* Then I said, "It's worth a try. We haven't got anything to lose." I hoped I sounded less skeptical than I felt.

Dr. Gale had a couple of keepers run ahead and open the door to the jaguar's cage. He organized the rest of us into two lines so that we formed a corridor through which she would walk. Then he took the dangerous position. He began to slowly put pressure on her by moving closer and closer. She snarled and swiped but he stood his ground. Finally she began to move. He applied constant and even pressure, not enough to challenge her but not so little that she would stop. The plan went so smoothly that the scene began to look like a man out for a walk with his pet jaguar. But the most difficult moment was still ahead: Would she go easily through the door to her cage?

Not only did she go easily; she actually became excited and ran to get back in her cage. This defied reason and logic.

Something inside of me had told me that she wanted her freedom, and that hadn't been the case at all.

I couldn't help but admire Dr. Gale's courage, but I was more intrigued with how he seemed to know that the jaguar would return to her cage willingly. So I asked him, "How did you know what she would do?"

His answer was great: "Well, you never know for sure what a wild animal will do and that's why we call them wild. But you can make a good guess based on Heine Hediger's book, *Psychology and Behavior of Animals in Zoos and Circuses.* Hediger's thesis is that an animal's perspective changes as soon as he leaves his territory or home—his cage, if you will. He quickly senses that he has nowhere to run. He has no sense of his surroundings; to him it's unfamiliar territory. He becomes insecure. Home represents security, so it becomes the desired destination."

"Would this method of recapturing an animal always be the best choice?" I questioned.

"I stay away from 'always' answers, but I do believe it's usually the best method to try first."

• • •

As important as Dr. Gale was to the return of the jaguar, the capture of the animal was successful only because a group of men stood together. They had lined up on both sides of the cat, keeping the chances of further escape to a minimum. The unified effort also provided for the safety of not only the zoo patrons but also each of the men involved. Dr. Gale could never have returned the jaguar to her cage alone. Teamwork got the job done.

The Lord is pleased when He sees His saints working together in unity as well. No one of us carries on the work of ministry alone. We were designed to cooperate as a team, much like the different parts of our bodies function as a team—an illustration the apostle Paul uses in 1 Corinthians chapter 12.

Philippians 2:2-4 defines what teamwork is all about. May you make Paul's encouragement a part of your own life today and always: "Complete my joy by being of the same mind, having the same love, being in full accord and of one mind. Do nothing from selfishness or conceit, but in humility count others better than yourselves. Let each of you look not only to his own interests, but also to the interests of others."

Chapter Six

I Never Realized

The arrival of a new rhinoceros at the Los Angeles Zoo turned out to be one of the most meaningful spiritual events in my life. Let me tell you about it.

One of the goals of a modern zoo is reproduction, especially of rare animals. This goal could not be realized with our black rhino collection because we owned only one male, Arthur (King Arthur). He was a young, robust, jaunty, temperamental male. But he needed a lady. We came through in a big way by our purchase of Lady Twinkle Toes, a dark, elusive beauty who pulsated with rhino charm.

When she arrived at the zoo, she was in a crate so large it could not be driven to the back of the exhibit because of the high bridges and tunnels that were a part of the back-road system. So the decision was made to lift the crate into the front of the exhibit with a large crane.

But then there was another problem: Lady Twinkle Toes was clearly upset. On that same day, her crate had been taken from the hold of a ship, lifted onto a truck, and driven 40 miles over the Los Angeles freeway system. The variety of smells, sounds, and shadows had taken their toll on an animal that is extremely subject to fear and anxiety. She was feeling more and more trapped by the crate and she wanted out. *Now!*

We knew this because she was repeatedly ramming the door of her massive crate so hard that we heard cracking and noticed splintering around the hinges. The order was shouted to hurry it up with the steel cables. There was a frenzy of activity as the cables were bolted together and attached to the giant hook at the end of the crane's cable.

"Lift away!" someone shouted. The crate began to rise amidst hoorahs and the diesel roar that thundered from the crane. Billows of smoke belched forth from an engine that obviously needed more maintenance. Inside the crate Lady Twinkle Toes had long since reached her stress limit. She was possessed by terror, and in her mind, her life was on the line. Her very survival was in question. Seventeen feet up from the ground, the crate began to rock violently. Four-by-fours bowed and cracked, and fell to the ground as the door began to disintegrate before our eyes. The crane operator swung the crate into position as quickly as possible while the rhino, with incredible strength, blasted the last vestiges of the door off its hinges.

We were terrified. If she attempted to jump from that height, she would be crushed and killed by her own weight. Rhinos see poorly, and she stared downward without the focus or intelligence to interpret her circumstances. She was trembling with fright and her eyes were filled with tears. Ten feet, eight feet, six feet, four feet. Still four feet above the ground, Lady Twinkle Toes opted for freedom. She fell with a sickening thud and we waited, with bated breath and clenched teeth, hoping she would be able to get up. She snorted and struggled successfully to a standing position. Her body was trembling violently with colossal fear, the kind that produces rage. She noticed a large boulder that, through tear-filled eyes, must have looked like a man or another animal. She charged it mightily. When she hit it, it moved only slightly and she fell to her knees. Staggering again to her feet, she noticed another boulder and charged it. Again the impact brought her to her knees. This time she got up a little more slowly. Then the most amazing thing happened . . . her whole body began to glisten red in the morning sun. She seemed to be perspiring great drops of blood from every pore in her body.

I turned to the veterinarian and exclaimed, "Doctor, what's going on? I have never seen anything like this before!"

"This animal has reached a maximum of stress," he said. "Rhinos, hippos, and elephants under this kind of stress can burst capillaries all over their bodies. She can't take much more stress. She's in great danger."

We were all glad when she stopped her awesome displays of fear and rage and began to calm down. As I considered this marvel, the words of another doctor, the beloved physician Luke, echoed in my mind.

> Being in anguish, [Jesus] prayed more earnestly, and his sweat was like drops of blood falling to the ground (Luke 22:44 NIV).

I thought, *Lord, I never realized. I never dreamed that You knew about stress in this way. How trapped You must have felt. How alone. You really can understand how I feel.*

The Lord impressed upon me two truths in this incident. It is good to reach out to friends during times of great stress. But when we don't come through to meet the need of a friend, God is always sufficient. He will get us through. Jesus is into stress management. We read this in Matthew 11:28-30:

> Come to me, all who labor and are heavy laden, and I will give you rest. Take my yoke upon you, and learn from me; for I am gentle and lowly in heart, and you will find rest for your souls. For my yoke is easy, and my burden is light.

Are you stressed? Take it to the Counselor first. Jesus understands.

Chapter Seven

Back-up Man

I always felt good about going into a cage with Bob Pedersen. He was the best back-up man in the business. I was sure that if something went wrong during a dangerous animal capture, Bob would be there to do whatever was needed to bail me out. He felt comfortable with my abilities, and we very much enjoyed working together.

When it is necessary to go into a cage and capture a potentially dangerous animal, the first rule of thumb is that there must always be two or more people to handle the animal effectively. The first man works the animal into position while the back-up man cuts off its avenues of escape. The roles can change back and forth when the animal moves around, but we usually decide who will catch and who will grab before we unlock the cage door.

Bob had excellent reaction time and he was strong. We netted and held everything from baboons to cheetahs, and neither of us ever sustained an injury when we worked together. In fact, the only time that I received any injuries was when I broke the cardinal rules of capture:

1) never go into a cage alone. 2) never work with an inexperienced back-up.

It was a lazy summer afternoon in August and I had finished all that I had been assigned around the health center. I needed to go down to the North American section to vaccinate the arctic foxes for distemper, hepatitis, and leptospirosis. They were overdue. I picked up the phone to call the section, then set it down again as a young and beautiful Ph.D. candidate from a local university walked into the health center office.

The woman glanced around, then asked me if there was anybody who could help her. I told her that I would if I could. She explained that she was doing a behavioral study on white-handed gibbon apes and needed to mark them with white paint so that she could readily tell which ape was which.

We drove down to the Eurasian section and I looked for the keeper who cared for the gibbons. He had already gone home for the day and I couldn't find anyone else who worked in the section. I noticed that the attractive young scientist kept checking her watch.

"Running late?" I queried.

"Yes, and I was so hoping that we would be able to get the marking done today," she replied. She sounded desperate—as if maybe she wouldn't get her Ph.D. or she would get an "F" on her assignment if she didn't get this task done.

"Well, I can't find anybody to do back-up, and I'm not supposed to go into a capture situation alone," I explained.

"I'm sorry to be putting you to so much trouble. Your gibbons must be more aggressive than the ones at the primate center. Ours were easy. I even helped. Hey, I would be glad to help you. I'll be your back-up."

"I'm sorry, I can't let you help. If you got bit, I'd get fired," I said.

She sat there looking so disappointed, so dejected. I had to prove that chivalry was not dead, so I made a stupid decision.

"I guess it wouldn't hurt anything to try," I announced.

"Oh, thank you, thank you, thank you. You're a dear."

Perhaps "dunce" would have been a more appropriate word, but just for a minute there I felt like a dear. And it felt good. I gathered the capture equipment together and carried it to the back of the gibbon cage. All three gibbons looked at the two hoop nets I was carrying and hooted their displeasure. Hand-over-hand they quickly retreated to the far end of the cage and huddled together for mutual comfort. They looked fairly intimidated, and I took that to be a good sign.

I entered the cage with confidence. I had learned to act confident whether I felt that way or not. It gave you a slight edge if the animals were on the defensive. I left one of the two nets leaning against the cage wall and began to make my advance. The apes headed in different directions and it looked like it would be every gibbon for itself. I made a beautiful pass of the net, and *whoosh!* I had a gibbon. I knew that my move must have looked impressive and I twisted the net to make sure that the gibbon wouldn't exit prematurely.

Right at that moment, the other two gibbons attacked me with a vengeance. I couldn't have engendered more wrath if I had tried. The two gibbons seemed to be coming at me from every direction at the same time. One got a large handful of my hair and decided to keep it. The other gibbon grabbed my arm with such force that he left a pronounced bruise. I wore it for more than a week.

There is no dignified way to exit a cage while being swarmed by gibbons. I just did the best I could to get out without being bitten to pieces. That was exactly what the Flying Gibbonski Brothers had in mind. As I fell backward into the holding cage, the beautiful young scientist had the presence of mind to push the sliding door shut. The gibbons continued to reach through the chain link, hoping to pull me back out where they could work me over good. But I had moved just out of their reach.

Now there is nothing clever that a person can say when he has just proven himself to be a jerk, but I went ahead and tried anyway.

"Well, Miss, do you think this might be why they recommend that we never go into a cage by ourselves?"

"Maybe so," she answered with a smile that convinced me that I had looked as ridiculous as I felt.

I would have been grateful if we could have just left and forgotten that the incident had ever happened. But there was still the little matter of the one gibbon that I had netted. It was still neatly bagged and lying quietly on the cool cement floor.

You can be sure your sins will find you out, I thought to myself.

I had no choice. I had to get someone to help me release the gibbon and retrieve the nets. I went and got my supervisor to come back with me, and together we quickly accomplished what I had failed to do alone.

"The next time you break the rules to impress somebody you may lose a finger, an eye, or your life. Don't do that anymore, Richmond," he said sternly.

We drove back to the health center silently, and I pondered my irresponsible actions. I never made that same mistake again, but I did make others.

We had just hired Dr. Reed, a new veterinarian who had just graduated from vet school. Dr. Reed had never worked with wild animals, and capture was something she had seen on television but had never participated in herself. She wanted to get some practice at capture, and because she was my supervisor, I felt obligated to indulge her request.

The animal she wanted to catch was an adolescent greater kudu. A kudu is one of the largest antelopes, and though this young male weighed only a little more than a hundred pounds, he could still do some serious damage with his formidable hooves. We agreed that Dr. Reed would make the initial grab and control the head, neck, and front legs. She had to keep the kudu from falling to the ground or it would be in a great position to kick somebody's head off. I was the back-up man, and my job was to control the hindquarters and keep the kudu on his back feet. That's because the hindquarters are the business end—the end that can deliver the most damage.

Dr. Reed rushed toward the kudu and exhibited a good deal of pluck as she grabbed the young animal. I grabbed the hindquarters and our veterinary intern began to inject a large dose of penicillin. It was then that Dr. Reed lost her grip, and in trying to regain it, she actually tipped the animal upside down.

The kudu kicked upward with all of its might and knocked me unconscious for a moment. The hoof had passed through my open mouth and connected with the rear teeth on the opposite side of my head. My gums were bleeding profusely and, when I regained consciousness, all I could hear was a loud ringing in my ears.

When things began to make sense again, I heard Dr. Reed saying, "Tell me where you are. Tell me your name." After I had convinced her that I had fully returned to coherency, I was whisked away for medical treatment.

After that I decided that I would never again work without an experienced back-up or lead person. I stuck to that decision for the last two years of my zoo career, and to my memory, I was never injured in a capture situation again.

• • •

In life, there is great wisdom in surrounding ourselves with people who will provide good back-up. They will pull us out of trouble when we get into a mess. They will remind us that we are out of line and need to be playing by the rules. They will pour courage into us so that we can perform to the limits of our potential.

Because we reap what we sow, it is necessary that we learn to be good back-up people ourselves. The following is a list of the qualities found in a good back-up person. If you have learned to love yourself and put yourself first, then you need not apply for this position because it requires a willingness to sacrifice self and courage enough to live for others.

You'll notice as you read through the following list that the Christian version of back-up is appropriately called *one anothering*. As you read, you'll want to think of people in your life who are good at watching out for you and others.

John 15:12—Love one another.
Romans 5:13—Don't pass judgment on one another.
Romans 12:5—Be members of one another.
Romans 12:10—Be devoted to one another.
Romans 12:10—Honor one another.
Romans 12:16—Live in harmony with one another.
Romans 14:19—Build up one another.
Romans 15:5—Be like-minded toward one another.
Romans 15:7—Accept one another.
1 Corinthians 6:6—Don't pursue lawsuits against one another.
1 Corinthians 12:25—Care for one another.
Galatians 5:13—Serve one another in love.
Galatians 5:15—Don't spitefully hurt one another.
Galatians 5:26—Don't provoke or envy one another.
Galatians 6:2—Bear one another's burdens.
Ephesians 4:32—Be kind to one another.
Ephesians 4:32—Forgive one another.
Ephesians 5:21—Submit to one another.
Colossians 3:9—Don't lie to one another.
Colossians 3:13—Teach and counsel one another.
1 Thessalonians 3:12—Abound in love toward one another.
1 Thessalonians 4:18—Comfort one another.
Titus 3:3—Don't hate one another.

Hebrews 3:13—Encourage one another.
Hebrews 10:24—Stir up one another to love and good deeds.
James 4:11—Don't slander one another.
James 5:9—Don't bear grudges against one another.
James 5:16—Confess your sins to one another.
James 5:16—Pray for one another.
1 Peter 4:9—Offer hospitality to one another.
1 Peter 5:14—Greet one another.
1 John 1:7—Have fellowship with one another.

Now that you know the qualities of a good back-up person, try to think of the people in your life who fill that role for you. Why don't you write or call them and thank them? They deserve it.

Look through the list again. Do you see any qualities that are among your strengths and that you use to support others? What are some of the qualities you could improve?

Why don't you take a moment now to thank God for the back-up people in your life? Thank Him also for the opportunities you have had to serve as a back-up person for others, and ask Him to help you grow in the areas that you would like to improve.

CHAPTER EIGHT

Easy to Grab, Hard to Let Go

Don't you just hate king cobras? I know I do—and I came by my feeling honestly. Our zoo had a thirteen-foot giant that seemed, to me, to be the embodiment of evil. He had a scar over his left eye that made him look mean and, more significantly, kept him from shedding his skin in a normal fashion. At least twice a year we would get the dreaded phone call from the reptile house: "The cobra shed his skin last week, but the eye cap didn't come off. It looks infected. Do you suppose you and the doc could come down and clean it?"

A snake's skin includes a clear scale over the eye to protect it from sand and foreign objects. Snakes have no eyelids, so they have no way to blink for protection. Our king cobra's scar prevented a normal shed, so the eye cap needed to be surgically removed.

We made the appointment for the next day. The arrangements for this procedure were critical because of the extreme danger involved. Only two people at the zoo could take responsibility for grabbing the more deadly snakes, and this was the most deadly. This snake's venom glands contain enough poison to kill one thousand adults—a fact that seemed to come up every time we did this procedure.

The curator of reptiles was assigned to grab the head, and two reptile keepers were to steady the body. When the snake was subdued, the veterinarian would begin the delicate surgery. His arena kept him inches from a lethal injection. My job was to furnish the scalpel, sponge, hemostat, and anything else necessary to expedite the surgery.

The capture of the cobra was as follows: The five of us took our positions. The two keepers stood on either side of the large cage door. The curator stood in front of the door about six feet away. The vet and I stood on either side of the curator about ten feet from the door. The keepers' only defense were sheer bird nets with two-foot handles.

With a nod of his head, the curator signaled for the door to be opened. Seconds later the king cobra appeared. As soon as he saw us, he stopped, spread his cape, and raised himself to full stature. The cage was two feet off the ground, so we were all looking at the snake at eye level. The cobra was trembling with excitement as he, in turn, looked back at each of his five enemies. He seemed to be choosing who would be his prey. The curator was chosen, and with shocking quickness the snake lunged forward, hissing and growling with malevolent rage. With lightning speed, the skilled keepers placed the sheer nets over the snake's head. And as he pushed to get through, the curator firmly grasped his neck just behind the venom sacs. The keepers grabbed the writhing body, then the curator nodded and said, "Let's get this over with."

The pressure was incredible. The vet's hands were trembling and beads of sweat began to run down the curator's forehead. The curator turned to me and asked, "Do you have any cuts or scratches on your hands?"

I looked and said, "No."

"Get a wad of paper towels, quick," he said in a strained voice. I did so.

"Now, put the wad in the cobra's mouth."

The cobra watched the paper towels as they were carefully positioned to allow him to bite them. He bit down violently and began to chew. The towels became yellow with venom until they began to drip.

The curator continued, "Did you know several elephants die every year from king cobra bites? A man could never survive a bite with a full load of venom. That's why I'm having you drain his venom sacs. My hands are sweaty and my fingers are cramping. When I let him go, it may not be quick enough. More people are bitten trying to let go of snakes than when they grab them. You get weak quickly when you grab a big poisonous snake."

• • •

There are many situations in life that are like catching and holding onto a poisonous snake—situations that are easy to grab and hard to let go. And oftentimes, it's not until we've become weakened that we realize we've endangered ourselves. Perhaps you're holding onto seemingly harmless serpents such as indebtedness, jealousy, anger, a desire for vengeance, gossip, lying, or hatred. Don't fool yourself; these can cause a lot more damage than we realize. Or perhaps you're tangling with other serpents like promiscuity, pornography, or substance abuse.

These and many more are serpents that will drain your strength and bite you when you try to let them go. Scripture warns us, "There is a way which seems right to a man, but its end is the way of death" (Proverbs 14:12).

You may be waking up to the fact that you're too weak to let go of something you're holding onto. This can happen to any of us. Please ask for help—seek out a pastor, a godly friend, a professional counselor, or a physician. We are fortunate to live in a world where help is available.

It pays to think carefully before we grab onto something that can hurt us. Are you embracing something that's exciting but harmful? Then you'll want to let it go—the sooner, the better.

Chapter Nine

You'd Better Sit Down

I was preparing a surgical pack in the zoo's well-stocked operating room when I was called to the phone. "Richmond, I hear the vets are at a conference and won't be back until this afternoon." I recognized the voice of the senior keeper at the children's zoo.

"That's right, Bill. Is something up?"

"Yeah! We have these raccoon kittens down here and they are both showing signs of losing the use of their hind legs. It's the darndest thing. We've never seen anything like this."

"Would you like me to pick them up? I could keep them up here until the vets get back from the conference. They will probably need to do some testing and take X-rays anyway."

"That would be great, Richmond. Then if they have something hot they won't be passing it around down here. Let's go for it."

I drove right down and picked them up. It was about 9:30 in the morning. I took them out of their carrying cage when I got back to the health center and confirmed that they were indeed losing the use of their hind legs.

Raccoon kittens are extremely appealing. These had been hand-raised and were both playful and affectionate. They seemed all right except for the extreme weakness in their hind legs, so I placed them in the two large pockets of my lab coat. As I puttered from room to room I played with the little bandits. They loved to chew on my fingers and wrestle with my hands. But they soon tired and napped a good deal more than normal. When they woke they refused to eat and played a bit less enthusiastically than they had in the morning. I felt sorry for them, so I stayed in contact with them the whole day long.

It was about four o'clock when the veterinarians returned. Dr. Bill Hulsizer came in first. He found me in the X-ray room, and the color drained from his face when he saw the raccoon kittens in my pockets.

"Are they losing the use of their legs?" he asked in a most serious tone.

"How'd you know? You haven't even looked at them," I declared in genuine astonishment.

He lifted the young raccoons out of my pockets and placed them onto a bath towel in a stainless steel cage. "You'd better sit down, Gary. You're not going to be too happy about what I'm going to tell you."

I sat down wondering what I had done wrong. I couldn't think of anything, but that didn't stop me from wondering.

He looked me right in the eye and said, "I'm about 90 percent sure both of the kittens have rabies."

"What?" I exclaimed in disbelief. "How could you know? You haven't even examined them."

Bill then proceeded to tell me a story that surprised and hurt me. He shared that our other veterinarian, Dr. Westfall, had given the raccoon kittens a modified live rabies vaccine as what she thought should be a standard procedure to protect them. She did not realize that, even though it prevents rabies in dogs, such a vaccine can *cause* rabies in raccoons. Bill said that he had discovered this serious error while he was reviewing the medical records at the children's zoo. He had confronted Dr. Westfall immediately, and she was embarrassed about her lack of knowledge. She insisted that she would handle the situation her own way and asked Bill to back off as if he didn't know a thing. Unfortunately, that's exactly what he did. She had discovered a statistic that indicated that there was a chance the raccoons would not come down with rabies at all, so she decided to play the odds. She even went as far as erasing the medical records at the children's zoo. Both vets checked the raccoons two to three times a day, but they never mentioned anything to me. They didn't count on the raccoons coming down with rabies the one day that they were both away at a conference.

"How can you be sure they have the disease?" I challenged. "They're not foaming at the mouth."

"They have the more common symptoms—what we call the mute form of the disease."

"Does this mean that I will have to go through the series of shots that I've always heard about?" I asked.

"That depends on whether or not you have experienced vital contact. If you have been bitten or your skin has been broken or scratched, that is vital contact. If you have any open sores that their saliva might have entered that would be vital contact. In the case of the baby raccoons, it would be considered vital if they so much as scratched you because these little guys put their paws in their mouths so much. Let's see your hands."

My hands were covered with nicks and scratches, about half of which they had caused that day. Bill nodded and said, "I think you'll want to take the treatment."

I felt sick. I would now be finding out if the treatment was worthy of its horrible reputation.

The raccoon kittens were sacrificed and their brains were sent to two different labs for analysis. Both labs confirmed rabies. A thorough investigation was launched to determine who might have sustained vital contact with the raccoons. One hundred and twenty people had been exposed, but only five in a vital way. There were two children's zoo attendants, the zoo's photographer and his assistant, and me. One of the children's zoo attendants refused to take the treatment for personal reasons, so, as it turned out, only four of us met to take the hard road together.

Forty hours after exposure we were driven to County General Hospital. The first matter of business was to determine if we were strong enough to endure the treatment. They gave each of us a thorough physical, and we all proved to be of sound body. Then they told us that three percent of the people who took the treatment died from it. Of course each of us thought we might be in that three percent, and one of us was nearly correct.

We were given other statistics that spelled out our chances. If we were punctured by a rabid animal there was a 50-50 chance that we would come down with the disease. If we came down with the disease, there was a 100 percent chance that we would die from it. We were also warned that one out of the four of us might experience a violent allergic reaction to the massive dose of horse serum we were about to receive.

Then the treatment began. They decided that my dose of horse serum would be 50 cc.'s. The syringe and needle looked like an outlandish prop from a bizarre comedy, but let me assure you that it was not funny. I hope I shall never receive that large a dose of anything ever again. It hurt tremendously, and sitting down was out of the question for hours to come.

They led us into another room and we began the series to the abdominal area. They chose that area because we use the least amount of muscles there. Rabies shots, in addition to being painful, are also somewhat complicated. First, a map is drawn to direct where the doctor will administer the shots. He writes the numbers 1 through 23 right on the abdomen in indelible ink. That way he will not give the shots in the same place twice. The shots are carefully administered subcutaneously (between the muscles and the skin). Then the swelling begins and the severe soreness sets in.

Shots one and two were given. They were very painful. The burning pain lasted about two minutes and gave way to soreness and intense itching. But it was bearable, and we began to encourage each other during each administration.

We met at the zoo every morning and were driven to the hospital. The hospital was not an architectural triumph, and it resided in a depressed area of Los Angeles. It seemed grey, gloomy, and institutional, especially stark after leaving the gardenlike atmosphere of the zoo in Griffith Park.

The four of us became good friends and determined that we ought to make the best of a bad thing. We would all take turns pretending to foam at the mouth and trying to bite one of the others. I shared that this experience would be great to tell our grandchildren in years to come—it may even make a good story for a book someday. When I discovered that my blood was going to be valuable and could be sold after I completed the treatment, I was overjoyed. I shared my discovery with the others the next morning. Karen, the children's zoo attendant that was with us, said, "Gary, you're making this sound like we have just had one big stroke of luck. It's not that good."

Karen was not at the zoo to meet us for our fifth day of treatment. She had been admitted to the hospital the night before. So after we received our ninth and tenth shots, we went up to her room to see her. She was covered with a fiery red rash and her face was very puffy. We managed to cheer her up some, but all of us were finding it hard to be good little soldiers. The course of treatment was making us all tired. I had a constant headache and was nauseous most of the time. We were all experiencing a good deal of swelling and itched fiercely all of the time. The doctors said that these symptoms were good signs. It meant that our bodies were fighting the virus. I knew my body was fighting back, but I wished it was not the battleground as well.

I was not up to working on the sixth day and my wife, Carol, insisted on driving me straight to the hospital. On the way my fingers began to swell and hives began to appear everywhere. The doctors were a bit concerned, but they felt that the symptoms could be controlled with medication. So they let me go home.

A few hours later Carol drove me back to County General, and they admitted me quickly. The medication hadn't helped at all.

I was becoming ill with a ravaging case of serum sickness. The swelling progressed until I was unrecognizable. I couldn't bend my fingers and it was painful to touch anything. The itching was fiery and incredible. No pain that I have ever encountered before or since compares to the sensations that I felt during that 24 hours of hell. I felt trapped in the dimensions of my own body. There is not a torture chamber on earth that could have punished me more severely. It was difficult to breathe, and I was racked with nausea and retching constantly. I stayed coherent during the whole ordeal and saw the concerned looks on the doctors' faces in the intensive care unit. I knew that I was in trouble and prayed constantly for relief. I repeated the name of Jesus over and over and I felt His presence with me.

I thought that I might be dying and I was afraid. I wasn't so afraid for myself, but I didn't want to leave Carol alone with our two little girls, Marci and Wendi. I begged the Lord to make the feelings go away, but they didn't.

I watched the hospital clock from my position on the gurney. Minutes seemed like hours, and hours seemed like years. It got to a point where the pain was so intense that I lost my resolve to live. I prayed, "Take me, Lord, and I'll trust You to take care of my family." I really wanted to die, but still the night went on. I thought about the great saints and remembered Job. His trials had lasted nearly a year, and he had continued to hang in there. I remembered Jeremiah, who had come to the end and proclaimed that the Lord was his sufficiency. Then I remembered the apostle Paul and what he had written to the church at Philippi:

> . . . that I may know Him and the power of His resurrection, and may share His sufferings, becoming like Him in His death (Philippians 3:10).

A tremendous peace settled in as I realized I had been given a chance to know Christ in a different way than I had ever known Him before. He had suffered because of my sin, and now I was suffering because of someone else's sin. We had something in common now, and it helped me to know something about His powers of love that added to His greatness. He chose to suffer for me before I had loved Him in any way. There were only a handful of people I would be willing to suffer for, and all of them already loved me. How different Jesus was from me. How better. How perfect.

I resigned to the will of Jesus and He waited there with me.

I asked to talk to my wife in case it would be the last time I would get the chance. I was getting weaker by the minute. I told her that I wanted her to know that I loved her. She knew something was probably really wrong because I tend not to say that nearly as much as I should.

By morning there was a blessed relief that let me know that I was going to live. I thanked the Lord.

Dr. Westfall never apologized for her actions that almost cost us our lives, but I still forgave her gladly and freely because of what Jesus taught me during our night of horrors together.

> Since we are justified by faith, we have peace with God through our Lord Jesus Christ. Through him we have obtained access to this grace in which we stand, and we rejoice in our hope of sharing the glory of God. More than that, we rejoice in our sufferings, knowing that our suffering produces endurance, and endurance produces character, and character produces hope, and hope does not disappoint us, because God's love has been poured into our hearts through the Holy Spirit which has been given to us (Romans 5:1-5).

Now that's Good News.

Chapter Ten

Free as a Bird

It didn't make sense to me. The criminals were as free as a bird and the birds were in jail. It probably won't make sense to you either. Let me explain.

When I was first transferred to the zoo health center, I found myself caring for a cage full of red-tailed hawks. There were 15 of them, and they were crowded together in a pitifully small cage. To my eye, they looked very depressed. I asked why we were caring for 15 red-tailed hawks off-exhibit, and the answer really frosted me.

The senior keeper, an extremely jovial Mexican-American man by the name of Johnny Torres, said "Eeeeeeh, those hawks are evidence for court trials. Some people caught them illegally and we keep them here until their trial is over."

"What happens when the court trials are over?" I asked.

"I don't know," he answered. "We never hear. Some of these birds have been here a long time. We don't even know which bird goes with what trial. So they'll probably die here."

"That doesn't make sense to me," I protested.

"Richmond, did somebody lie to you and tell you things make sense around here? It's best not to ask too many questions about this either. The guys down below, down in administration, they don't like to know that they got problems. So my advice is to drop it."

Well, it just wasn't in my nature to drop it. After all, this was injustice pure and simple. The poachers were free and the poachees were being punished.

I inquired around gently and in time became convinced that the birds were in trouble. Nobody cared about their plight, and the red tape to get them released was so sticky that no one would wade through it.

There was really only one answer. They had to be set free. But it had to look like an accident. The punishment for letting out low-risk animals was nothing more than a notice to correct a deficiency. I had never received one before, but I figured it would be a small price to pay to right this wrong.

I decided that I would let the birds go on a Tuesday afternoon when the supervisors were at the animal health committee meeting. They would be gone from the area for about two hours—more than enough time to accomplish my mission.

Tuesday came and the supervisors left the hospital area. I made my way out to the cage, slipped the lock out of the hasp, and left the door wide open. I looked around. There was no one in sight. I slipped back into the health center and set about my duties with a profound sense of fulfillment, an abiding feeling of satisfaction. It was not to last.

After one hour I decided to check the cage. Astonishment, disbelief, wonder, and confusion reigned supreme as I beheld all 15 hawks relaxing in the cage. There was still time to get them out; perhaps they just needed some inspiration. Well, I knew what would inspire them: I ran into their cage waving my arms and growling like a bear. That inspired them, all right. They flew out of the cage and landed not ten feet from the door. The look that they gave me was pitiful. They were confused and it was clear to me that they wanted back into the cage.

"Don't you see the sky?" I pleaded. "That's what you were meant for." I began feeling a little self-conscious inside the cage, so I stepped out to finish my address.

"What's wrong with you? You're not chickens. You're majestic birds of prey. You hunt your food. God gave you a purpose; now go fulfill it."

I decided to go back to the health center. Maybe their instincts would take over and they would feel some primal urge to command the wind. I left for 15 minutes and then returned. Not one bird had felt any urges. In fact, some had walked back into the cage.

With 15 minutes left to go, I gave up. I don't mind telling you I was more than a little deflated. I rounded up the birds like a herd of goats and put them back into the cage.

Where had I gone wrong?

I had approached their problem anthropomorphically, which is a fancy way of saying I was projecting my thoughts into the minds of the birds. The birds had not been sitting in the cage longing to be free. Those were my thoughts. They had long since become satisfied with just waiting to be fed. No famines to suffer. No droughts to survive. No territorial battles to enjoin. It wasn't all bad. I felt bad, but they didn't.

The reason I felt bad was because by caging them, we had taken something from them that they needed to be noble—their purpose. God had created the red-tailed hawks to hunt rodents and reptiles. Few birds can equal their elegant flight or fearless pursuit of prey. This group of birds had been robbed of their ecological purpose. What's more, we weren't even letting the zoo patrons appreciate them. That bothered me.

I thought a bit more about freedom as I finished my responsibilities that day. I concluded that freedom was the ability to fulfill the purpose for which you were created. I further reasoned that man had an interesting distinction. Unlike the animals, he can never be kept from fulfilling his purpose. He is always, in every circumstance, free to perform the function for which he was created. Man's purpose is to love and serve God. The more difficult the circumstances, the greater the opportunity to achieve that purpose. We are now and will always be free to be what we were meant to be . . . that creature designed to glorify God and enjoy Him forever.

Solomon, the wisest man who ever lived, put it this way:

> The end of the matter; all has been heard. Fear God, and keep his commandments; for this is the whole duty of man. For God will bring every deed into judgment, with every secret thing, whether good or evil (Ecclesiastes 12:13-14).

The apostle Paul shares this in Galatians 5:

> For freedom Christ has set us free. . . . For you were called to freedom, brethren; only do not use your freedom as an opportunity for the flesh, but through love be servants of one another (verses 1, 13).

Are you fulfilling the purpose for which you were created? Or have you become satisfied with the ways of the world?

You have the freedom to choose.

CHAPTER ELEVEN

Ladybug

When I was seven our family got a small black and tan puppy and named her Ladybug. I do not recall where we got her, but even after more than 30 years have come and gone I can vividly recall the warmth of her head lying across my bare feet and the look of love in her eyes as she watched to see if she would be invited on any adventure that led her beyond the boundaries of our yard. She was an ardent traveler and loved to ride in the car. No dog ever born enjoyed more the wind whipping her ears and flapping her lips as she leaned as far as we would permit out the back window of our '53 Chevrolet station wagon.

Ladybug weighed in at about 15 pounds, maybe 20, and the consensus was that she was a cross between a cocker spaniel and a beagle. She was a happy dog and ticklish. If you scratched her in just the right place she actually smiled. Now I know that's hard to believe, but, hang it all, she smiled, and if you saw it you would call it that too.

When I was young I actually thought of Ladybug as a member of the family. To me she was the youngest child,

Ladybug Richmond. She slept with us, and many was the morning that I was licked awake. Between the ages of seven and nine I never washed my ears because Ladybug did it for me almost every morning.

She did have a fault that remained with her all the days of her life. She had breath that you could see on a warm day. Whatever doggy breath is, she had twice as much as should be allotted. We had to apologize for it more than once. She was also possessed of a great capacity for natural gas production and could not contain it.

Ladybug was my friend and shadow and I always loved her—but never more than the one summer day that I asked for and obtained her forgiveness. Here is what happened.

I was raised in Altadena, California, a small friendly town nestled against the San Gabriel Mountains. You have seen these very mountains if you have watched the Rose Parade or the Rose Bowl football game. The San Gabriels watch over Pasadena and Altadena and most of the Los Angeles basin. Now Altadena had much to commend it, but right up there at the top, smack dab in the middle of the "amen corner" was Kern's Delicatessen. Old Mr. Kern had located some of the finest culinary delights known to the palates of our species. His Swiss cheese, pumpernickel bread, and kosher dill pickles were the best. It was a four-block walk to the deli, but I would make the walk anytime some benefactor would finance the pilgrimage.

One very hot summer afternoon in deep August I had a little extra cash and remembered how much I enjoyed biting into one of Mr. Kern's renowned kosher dills. I was with a friend, Doug Sigler, and asked if he would like to walk to Kern's with me. As it turned out, my brother and a friend of his decided to go also. When we got to the front door of our house, Ladybug was wiggling with delight for she was sure we were going to let her come along. After a little banter we agreed and were out the door on our way to the gates of heaven.

Ladybug was not leashed because she would never bite anyone. She was always bounding just ahead, stopping now and then to smell something and make a memory. She would run over and jump on us now and then to let us know she was glad to be part of the adventure. Ladybug was five going on six at the time, and I was going into the seventh grade in the fall.

When we arrived at Kern's, we told Ladybug to sit at the front door and wait for us while we ate inside. I purchased one piece of his pumpernickel bread, one slice of aged Swiss cheese, one large kosher dill pickle, and a bottle of Dad's Old-Fashioned Root Beer. Life doesn't get better than eating at Kern's Delicatessen with family and friends. We left only after licking our fingers clean; leaving anything uneaten would have been a sin.

Once outside we ordered Ladybug to follow us home. Twenty steps down the street we looked into the Hillcrest Pharmacy window and noticed the latest issue of *Mad* magazine. We again ordered Ladybug to sit on the sidewalk and wait while we went into the store. We read *Mad* over my friend's shoulder and laughed at the absurd humor. Laughter's tears streamed down our faces. The store clerk asked us to buy or fly, so we left. We left a little embarrassed and miffed. We also left through the back door, which provided a shortcut home. Ladybug, however, continued to wait patiently at the front door of Hillcrest Pharmacy.

On the way home we groused over being given the bum's rush at the pharmacy. The afternoon began to blend with evening, and our friends both left for home and dinner. My dad came home from a hard day's work in construction and, after washing up, called us to the dinner table. It was a meat-and-potatoes meal and we had a lot of the kind of leftovers a family dog would kill for. My father scraped them onto a plate and stepped out the back door to call for Ladybug.

She didn't come.

Dad came back into the house and asked Steve and me if we had seen her, and we both looked at each other. I didn't know for sure what Steve was going to do, but I was trying to figure out a way to blame our thoughtless mistake on him. I refused to answer, hoping that if my brother spoke first he would get most of the blame for losing our dog. Steve finally admitted that we had left her outside the pharmacy. My Dad had a disgusted look, which he administered pretty equally as I remember. He told us to jump in the car, and we backed out of our driveway a lot faster than usual. He didn't say much, but he did inquire if we had traded our brains for sawdust. We knew well that we had better not answer that particular question. If we said no, we were smart-mouthing. If we said yes, we were smart-mouthing. So we both did what he wanted us to do; we looked guilty and stupid and kept quiet. (Now I don't know what you're thinking, but I don't agree with the notion that there are no appropriate times for a tongue-lashing. God did it all the time to Israel, and Jesus did it to His disciples. Steve and I were getting less than we deserved, and I knew it even then.)

My father knew enough about dogs to know that Ladybug was capable of following her own scent home, so he followed the route we had walked to the delicatessen. The farther we drove without seeing her the worse I felt. I had let down one of my best friends and I knew it. I had a lump in my throat as I began to picture my dog run over by a car or cringing in the back of a cage at the dog pound. We finally rounded the corner of Mariposa Lane and Lake Street and saw a small dark form curled into a ball by the front door of the pharmacy. Steve stuck his head out the window and yelled, "Here, girl!"

His yell awoke Ladybug, and she bounced against the glass thinking we were still in the store. Steve left the car and picked her up.

I have never witnessed a more emotional reunion. Ladybug wiggled until I thought she would fall apart. She whined happily all the way home and licked every hand that came within a foot of her.

My father, happy about the outcome, said, "All's well that ends well, but don't you two ever let that happen to your dog again. I don't have to tell you all the bad things that could have happened to her, do I?" We nodded.

That night I asked Ladybug if she wanted to sleep with me. Her tail wagged as she ran ahead of me and jumped up on the bed. When I turned out the light, I called her to come close and I hugged her and told her how sorry I was to have let her down. She just kissed me and rolled over to have me scratch her tummy. I did that until we both fell asleep.

Ladybug was always anxious to forgive. Her only desire was that she be part of a family, our family, her family. The saying that dogs are man's best friends really isn't so far off in my experience.

• • •

You know what made me remember this story? I was reading about the prodigal son in the fifteenth chapter of Luke. It is my favorite story in the Bible. As I thought about the father, I was impressed by how anxious he was to forgive and be reunited to his son. The story answers the question, How does God feel when we are off blowing it? He is simply longing and waiting for us to come to our senses and come home. He is always, as my dog was with my brother and me, glad for the reunion.

If you have been away from God for awhile and you want to know how He feels, read the following account from Luke 15:11-24. If you want to know what to do about it, follow the prodigal son's lead and come home just as he did.

> There was a man who had two sons. The younger one said to his father, "Father, give me my share of the estate." So he divided his property between them.
>
> Not long after that, the younger son got together all he had, set off for a distant country and there

squandered his wealth in wild living. After he had spent everything, there was a severe famine in that whole country, and he began to be in need. So he went and hired himself out to a citizen of that country, who sent him to his fields to feed pigs. He longed to fill his stomach with the pods that the pigs were eating, but no one gave him anything.

When he came to his senses, he said, "How many of my father's hired men have food to spare, and here I am starving to death! I will set out and go back to my father and say to him: Father, I have sinned against heaven and against you. I am no longer worthy to be called your son: make me like one of your hired men." So he got up and went to his father.

But while he was still a long way off, his father saw him and was filled with compassion for him; he ran to his son, threw his arms around him and kissed him.

The son said to him, "Father, I have sinned against heaven and against you. I am no longer worthy to be called your son."

But the father said to his servants, "Quick! Bring the best robe and put it on him. Put a ring on his finger and sandals on his feet. Bring the fattened calf and kill it. Let's have a feast and celebrate. For this son of mine was dead and is alive again; he was lost and is found." So they began to celebrate.

Chapter Twelve

Mrs. Bedlam

The keepers at the Los Angeles Zoo had a saying: "The zoo would be a great place to work if you could just keep the people out." Like any saying, it had a background. Allow me to illustrate.

You would think you could trust senior citizens to behave themselves at the zoo. They were normally our most cherished visitors. But one little old lady engineered a mission of mercy that created more bedlam than any single visitor in the zoo's history. She looked innocent enough. She wore a faded black dress under her full-length black wool coat, and she displayed a wide-brimmed black hat with a silk rose that looked like it had been run over by a bus. But somehow, she passed security and the ticket-takers with two shopping bags filled to the brim with rubber balls. They were all shapes, colors, sizes, and textures.

She had been to the zoo many times before and had concluded the animals were bored. In her opinion, she was carrying two bags of recreation.

She threw a ball into the sea lion pool, and I'm sure she felt affirmed as the most playful animal of the zoo pushed it back and forth. She threw them into the bear moats, and the bears ate them, as did the monkeys. We knew that because the rubber showed up undigested in their waste material. Many of the animals simply ignored them, but not our female black-maned lioness. The ball thrown into her moated area was made of a very hard, dark blue rubber. The lioness bit down on it so hard that it was impaled on her awesome right canine. No amount of clawing at the ball dislodged it, and the female became increasingly distressed. She rubbed her face on the ground hoping to drag it loose. Her muzzle began to drip blood and mud, and she was salivating profusely. The keeper knew his animal needed help, and he called the health center and begged us to come quickly. His lioness was in trouble.

Dr. Bradford was the veterinarian on duty. He was brand new—just out of school. He had never worked with a lion before. Upon arriving we noticed the keeper had managed to lock the lioness in her night quarters. Dr. Bradford leaned on the bars to get a better look at her problem. She hated people and never tolerated anyone touching her cage. Knowing this, I reached out to pull him away, but it was too late. The lioness lunged at his face and roared. Now a roar under any circumstance is impressive; but inside a small, concrete building, it is a major event. It rumbled through our bodies like thunder and we found ourselves momentarily paralyzed. We, of course, were expecting it. Our young veterinarian, however, wasn't expecting it, so he fainted. He lay on the cement floor for a few seconds. When he had again become coherent, he said something I will not quote in case children are reading this. The essence of his comment was that he now believed in lions.

I think he enjoyed shooting the lioness with the tranquilizer gun and would have enjoyed shooting the little old lady more, but we never saw her again. She did call the next day, though, to see if the animals enjoyed the rubber balls.

When she was told how we had to remove the rubber ball with a hacksaw, she hung up.

I think we all understood that her motives were pure, but she clearly demonstrated a human potential. She did the wrong thing for the right reason. She was sincere, but she was sincerely wrong. The effect was the same as doing the wrong thing for the wrong reason. She could not have caused any more trouble if she had intended to harm the lioness.

The elderly woman's problem was that she was acting beyond her sphere of authority. She had no permission to act at all. She took this matter into her own hands.

This is when we create the most problems for ourselves—when we take matters into our own hands and act outside of God's authority. Intentions don't cut it. You've probably heard the old cliche, "The road to hell is paved with good intentions."

Dietrich Bonhoeffer, in his book *Ethics,* makes an interesting observation: "The tree of knowledge of Good and Evil produced the ability to choose our own good or our own evil." Both choices may take us an equal distance from God. But we have a third alternative—God's will.

One of my favorite films is *The Sound of Music.* My favorite moment in the film is when Mother Superior asks Maria, "What is the most important thing you have learned at the abbey?" Maria humbly answers, "To find God's will and do it." God has given us His Word for a lamp to light the way. His will is not hidden. And His Scripture provides all the authority we need to act rightly.

David wrote, "I have laid up thy word in my heart, that I might not sin against thee" (Psalm 119:11). He learned to do that after feeling the full effects of taking matters into his own hands.

Let's stop and think about our lives. Have we sought God's will about the way we live? Or have we taken matters into our own hands? Perhaps we have good intentions, but maybe what we're doing isn't what's best for other people. If we're not sure, we'll want to find out . . . before we hurt ourself or someone else.

Chapter Thirteen

It Will Be Different for Me

Bandit was irresistible. No raccoon that ever existed had more natural "cute" than this 90-day-old bundle of mischief. When my neighbor Julie bought him at the pet store, she was sure they would be lifelong friends. Everywhere she went, he went—usually perched on her shoulder. Bandit's habit of holding Julie's cheeks in his paws and looking into her eyes with sparkling curiosity always melted her and solicited an affectionate kiss and hug. And he grew. Eighteen months passed and Bandit became a strapping 25-pound adolescent raccoon, still full of the dickens and only slightly less playful. He still loved affection, rode on shoulders, and seemed to be a one-raccoon advertisement that raccoons make great pets.

I mentioned Julie and Bandit to our zoo veterinarian one day and inquired as to why more people didn't keep raccoons as pets. His answer floored me. "They undergo a glandular change at about 24 months. After that, they become unpredictable, independent, and often attack their owners."

"Are there exceptions?" I inquired.

"None that I know of," he said thoughtfully.

"Then Julie is likely to be bitten?"

"Any time now, I should think," the doctor added with conviction.

Since a 30-pound raccoon can be equal to a 100-pound dog in a scrap, I felt compelled to mention the coming change to Julie. She sat and listened politely as I explained what an eminent world authority had shared with me concerning raccoons and their nature. I'll never forget her answer.

"It will be different for me . . . Bandit is different." And she smiled as she added, "Bandit wouldn't hurt me. He just wouldn't!"

Three months later, Julie underwent plastic surgery for facial lacerations sustained when her adult raccoon attacked her for no apparent reason. Bandit was released into the wild.

That happened about 15 years ago, and I've heard Julie's reply many times since: "But it will be different for me."

Rob, a 16-year-old boy, said, "I know what I'm doing. It's different for me. I know all about dosages and stuff. My dad is a pharmacist." Rob overdosed six months later and spent two months in a mental ward.

Judy, a 15-year-old girl, argued, "I know he's been around, but it's different with us. He really loves me. He really does." Judy is now 25 and living at home with her nine-year-old son. The son has never met his father.

Jerry, an 18-year-old college student, declared, "I'm different. A few drinks don't slow me down a bit." Jerry is dead now, and he took three friends with him when he drove off an embankment. They were all drunk.

Pat, a 35-year-old woman, contended, "My kids are different. They will be able to handle the divorce fine. I'll spend more time with them. Besides, my lover is great with kids." Pat divorced her husband and married her lover. She divorced again after he tried to kill her. The children haven't slept well for years and need to see a counselor weekly.

David, a 40-plus-year-old executive, reasoned, "Wow, she's beautiful! Her husband is away on a business trip. Nobody will know. It will be different, exciting, temporary." David ended up causing this man's wife to get pregnant. To avoid a scandal, he had the man killed. He felt compelled to marry the woman; then her baby died. David's life was never the same again. That incident caused members of his family to turn against him, and one of his children even tried to kill him. I'm sure he never dreamed that life would get so tangled. I'm sure he thought, *It will be different for me.* (You can find this executive's biography beginning in 2 Samuel 11.)

Let's take one step back and look at our lives. Are we in violation of some well-known axiom? Are our closest friends or relatives warning us about something? Are we in conflict with the clear teaching of the Scriptures?

If so, then we need to use great caution and say to ourselves, "Maybe it *won't* be different for me."

Chapter Fourteen

El Lobo

In 1966 it was possible to order a wolf pup and make a pet of it. In fact, you could keep just about any animal as a pet that's now found in a zoo, excepting hippos and rhinos and perhaps giraffes. I suppose if you lived in the right area, you might even be able to order those as well.

Wild animals as a rule don't make good pets, but that didn't stop thousands of aspiring animal trainers from ordering them so that they might master them, and, in doing so, impress their friends. It is for such a reason that a young couple answered an ad in the *Los Angeles Times* that read, "Wolf pups $175. Call 555-2891." They called the number and took down the address in Pasadena where the pups could be viewed.

When they knocked on the door, a man with a dark brown beard answered. He looked as though he had just arrived by dogsled. He asked them to come in and make themselves comfortable.

"Sit here on the couch and I'll bring the pups out to you," he said enthusiastically. "The mama don't take to strangers handlin' her babies. I don't want ya gettin' a bad impression of wolves from the mama. She's a great pet, but just for the missus and me. Ya know what I mean?"

The young couple nodded as the burly man in the red plaid Pendleton shirt disappeared. They were excited because they had talked about getting an unusual pet for a long time. This would just about eat up their savings, but, shoot, money was to spend anyway. And $175 was a good price for a wolf, if it was tame.

When the man reappeared he was holding three gray balls of fur. All of them were wagging their tails and whining joyfully. As soon as they were put on the floor, the little male made a beeline to the young couple and jumped up to be held. The wife picked him up and cuddled him against her cheek. He licked her ear as clean as a whistle before she held him out to get a good look at him. To the surprise of her husband, she said, "We'll take this one."

"That there male thinks he's a dog. Friendliest wolf I ever saw. His daddy is good with most folks, but there's a few he don't like, and they gotta watch out or he'll get 'em good. That pup's different though. Least ways he is now."

Neither of the couple was listening. They were hugging and petting and playing with a most unique puppy. The husband had wanted to bargain, but his wife had made that impossible. He reached in his pocket, counted out $175, and placed it in the smiling man's hand.

When they asked how a wolf might be cared for, the man told them to treat it just like a dog. "Feed it Purina Puppy Chow for the first year and after that just go for Purina Dog Chow. You might pour some bacon grease on his food now and then to make his coat shine, but that's about it. Wolves are just big dogs and don't need nothin' you wouldn't give a dog. Ya gotta watch them when they get big cause they're a lot of animal. That pup might make 200 pounds and that's no lie. If you don't have him pretty obedient when he's grown, he could be hard to control. He could get you in a lot of trouble. They do a bunch of teething, so you might want to buy him a gob of rawhide chew toys or bones from the butcher shop."

The young couple left more excited than they had ever been in their lives. The wife held the pup on her lap, and he proved to be a good traveler, sleeping most of the way home.

"What should we name it?" asked the husband as he reached over and patted the sleeping wolf pup.

"Something that sounds Alaskan," answered his wife, searching her mind for a name that fit the criterion.

"I read this story about a sled dog named Niki of the North," offered the husband.

His wife squinted, then smiled. "I like Niki. It sounds like an Eskimo boy who was brave and strong. Niki it is," she said, proud of her husband for being so well read.

They drove to the market and spent the rest of their savings on dog food, dog toys, and a dog bed. The checkout lady was fascinated by Niki and managed to get kissed several times while she hugged him. The young couple was experiencing one of the intoxicating aspects of owning an exotic pet. The attention you get from other people is overwhelming.

Niki's puppyhood was in most ways like that of any large dog you might purchase from a pet store. He was bright, and they were able to housebreak him in what must have been record time, although they don't keep records for that sort of thing. His teething wasn't normal, though. No amount of rawhide or butcher bones kept him from chewing other things. It seemed that the other things were always costly. The young couple didn't have a pair of shoes between them that was free from chew marks. Most of their furniture was either tattered, scratched, or splintered, but it didn't matter to them because they had bought it used and would replace it as soon as Niki was finished teething—if he ever finished teething.

Niki had two other bad habits. He was an instinctive digger. Their backyard was full of Niki's attempts to make a den. He seem compelled to try to den under their nicest plants. The backyard looked like a nuclear wasteland by the end of Niki's first week. The lawn was also in great distress from urine burns. Amazingly, Niki never seemed to go in the same place twice. It was if he hated green and was trying to put it out like a fire.

The young husband marveled at Niki's digestive tract. What a mystery! How Niki turned a 50 pound bag of dog chow into 100 pounds of waste matter was beyond his comprehension. On top of that, Niki was rapidly getting larger. At six months he was a staggering 100 pounds of teen wolf.

Niki was playful and loving to all, and only the couple's closest friends and relatives knew that he was a wolf. The neighbors were told he was a shepherd mix. One neighbor looked at Niki and said "Mixed with what?" The young wife, who had the better sense of humor, shrugged and answered, "I think we can rule out Chihuahua."

One evening the young couple needed to go shopping and decided to leave their pride and joy in the backyard, where, as usual, he was digging a den. They would be back in 45 minutes and digging seemed the lesser of the two evils—digging and chewing. The inside of the house was still in better shape than the yard. They stood on the back porch, and the young wife said, "Be a good boy, Niki. We'll be back in a little while with a treat." Niki looked up, and his soft gray eyes met their approving smiles with love. He looked a bit silly with moist dirt on his nose, and they laughed at him and left for the store, not knowing this would be the last time they would own this wonderful pet.

Niki had dug a much larger hole than they had noticed, and it led underneath the wooden fence into the next-door neighbor's backyard. Fifteen minutes after the couple left, Niki squeezed under the fence and explored the neighbor's yard. The neighbors had a cat, and when Niki saw it, he gave chase. It led him quickly to the front yard, and he passed several houses down the block before the cat ditched him, jumping into another backyard a half block away. This was the first time Niki had ever been away from home without a leash.

There were instincts running through the veins of this young wolf that had never found expression, until now. Hunting was one of them. An adult wolf can lope 30 miles in search of food in a day and not exhaust himself. Niki looked in both directions and decided to follow the setting sun. It was Sunday night and most families were eating dinner. No one on the block saw Niki leave. Niki settled into a trot and the blocks drifted by at about eight miles an hour. He would stop now and then to smell the scents left by other animals, but he never turned back. Something primal was taking over. He was looking for something, but he didn't know what it was. It must be just ahead.

Minutes became hours. He had traveled 12 miles from home. He satisfied his thirst when he discovered an active sprinkler and continued on.

Back home, a distraught young couple was systematically driving the streets and looking for Niki. The wife was hysterical in the same way she would be if they were looking for their child, which was exactly what Niki had become until they had one of their own. But during their search, they never came within six miles of the wolf. For weeks afterward, they checked the local animal shelters to no avail. It was sad. You could see that they were both brokenhearted.

Niki took a rest just outside the fence of a female collie in heat. After several attempts at digging in cement, he curled up and slept with his nose just under the gate. The collie licked his dirty muzzle clean, and he liked it a lot! It was his first contact with a female, and he wished he could get a good look at her.

At 5:00 the next morning, Niki was rudely awakened by a rival suitor who also wanted to meet this fragrant female.

It was a large dog, almost as large as Niki, and he was battle worn. He had scars in places where most dogs don't have scars, and, to boot, this was his neighborhood.

His lips curled into a fierce snarl and a growl rumbled forth designed to intimidate your average dog. Niki, however, was not your average dog. In fact, he wasn't a dog at all. He was *Canis lupis,* the wolf, and he answered the rival with a growl so low and menacing that the intruder backed up. The dog stared hard and long at the young wolf. His instincts revealed that Niki was different from any dog he had ever tangled with, but still, this was his territory and no newcomer would get off easy as long as he was in charge.

The dog raised the hair on his back and neck and slowly approached Niki. Niki's hair raised slowly, and he crouched to protect his long legs. He then assumed a springing position. Niki pulled back his lips, revealing his massive canines, and growled threateningly. The dog could see that nothing was going to cause the young wolf to give an inch.

With surprising force the neighborhood hound plowed into Niki, having age and experience on his side. Niki was strong; power and instinct were his shield. They blocked and fenced with their teeth flashing, and both made enough noise to wake every neighbor on the block. Lights went on and front doors began to open to see the titans at war. Neither the dog nor the wolf had yet made contact, but you would have thought they were tearing each other to pieces by the noise they were making.

Youth began to favor Niki as the older dog began to tire. He slipped. When he did, Niki went for and grabbed the dog's throat in his massive jaws. Niki shook him like a rag doll and then released him. The dog lay on the lawn in shock for a moment. When he got his wits about him, he exposed his neck to Niki, signaling that the battle was over. Niki could keep the female collie for himself.

That was not to be, however, for her owner had grabbed a garden hose and turned it on them full blast. Both the dog and Niki ran off in the darkness of the morning as the neighbors reentered their homes to steal at least another hour of sleep before getting ready for work. Most of them knew Sparky and his habit of picking fights with other dogs, but they had never seen him come anywhere near losing before. He got thrashed in this skirmish, and it didn't last a round. They all knew they had heard something fearsome, but none had any idea that they had heard the ancient sounds of the wolf in battle. It had been more than 150 years since that sound had echoed through this California suburb, it had been heard by Indians on their way to the San Gabriel Mission. That night, an Indian's dog was killed and never seen again.

Niki headed west and north. He found himself lost in the maze of streets that make up the rather exclusive town of San Marino. He was getting hungry and, having no fear of people, began to look in their backyards for dog food. At 8:30 A.M., a retired doctor shut the gate to his backyard, trapping Niki.

The old doctor called the Humane Society, and they came quickly to capture Niki. Niki took it all in stride. The animal control officer took special care with Niki because he was not convinced this animal was a dog. Niki wore a collar and was tame, but still he looked very much like a wolf should look. When Niki arrived at the shelter, several employees came to look at him and argue his origins. Some thought a shepherd mix, others argued husky or malamute, and a few expressed agreement with the officer who had picked up Niki. Indeed, this might be a wolf. Niki was wearing a collar, but he had no dog tag; a mistake that the young couple was to regret. They had nothing to tie themselves to this magnificent animal. They never dreamed he would run from Pomona to San Marino, 28 miles away, so they never checked that animal shelter. There was nothing on the collar, so, of course, there was no one for the shelter to call.

Niki had a month to be claimed; then he would be destroyed. The days ticked by. He was not a likely candidate for adoption because he looked so formidable, but the handlers liked him and continued to debate whether or not he was a dog. One of them went to the local library and brought in a book with several pictures of wolves. Niki looked very much like the pictures. The employees began to lean in unison toward the wolf theory, and the supervisor called the Los Angeles Zoo to ask if someone would please come and tell them what they were keeping. At that time, the zoo didn't have a good relationship with animal shelters and did not respond quickly. Niki's date for destruction was just two days off. Something needed to happen soon or a special animal would pass out of existence for no good reason. The head of the shelter called the zoo director, who had not heard of their request. Knowing that the zoo was in need of a male wolf, the director sent out a veteran senior keeper to make the call.

When he arrived at the shelter, he was met by 12 shelter employees who had argued for almost a month over Niki's origins. It took the senior keeper two seconds to say, "Friends, you've got a wolf, and we'd be more than glad to give him a good home. Where do I sign some papers to get him out of here?"

A cheer went up from the staff because they had prevented a needless act of destruction. Many children would enjoy this magnificent specimen of wolf for years to come. On the way back to the zoo, the senior keeper decided a tame wolf should have a name, so he scratched Niki behind the neck and said, "You look like a 'lobo' to me, so that's what I'm going to call you. I never got to name an animal at the zoo before, so I'm just going to tell them that's your name." The young wolf licked his hand as if to agree, and from that point on he was called Lobo, which is, as you probably already know, Spanish for wolf. When Lobo was let out of the zoo truck, he shook himself and leaned against the senior keeper for comfort. It was then that he heard a gentle whine and saw Missy. Missy was an elegant she-wolf. She had soft gray eyes that smiled at everybody. The entire time I knew her, about ten years, I never saw her show any signs of aggression. She was sweet, and, from the looks of it, Lobo was wondering if he was seeing an angel for the first time. If he could have said anything, most likely it would have been, "Is she really for me?"

The senior keeper smiled and said, "Yes, Lobo, she's going to be all yours as soon as the vet checks you out." Lobo trembled with excitement and made some whining sounds of his own. Now I don't understand wolf, but I think he was saying, "Soon won't be soon enough!" Lobo held Missy's gaze, and it was clearly love at first sight. Word was that there would be wolf pups next spring.

The vet muzzled Lobo so he could give him his shots. He didn't know that Lobo was well covered for distemper and rabies and even accustomed to a veterinarian's poking and prodding. Lobo loved everyone he met, and everyone loved him. He had found a new home where he would receive everything he needed to be happy, not the least of which would be a little Canadian sweetheart named Missy.

Much to Lobo's disappointment he was kept at the health center for two weeks because he needed treatment for worms. He was in perfect health except for that, and that posed no threat to him.

Lobo remembered his brief glimpse of Missy. Every morning, very early, he would howl to see if she would howl back. She did, and they both sounded miserable. At first they only howled in the morning, but then they began to howl most of the day. You can't imagine how annoying wolf howling gets when you hear it for hours at a time. Let me tell you—it's *real* annoying! We heard the patrons were loving it down in the zoo. Sure, they could get away from the continued piteous patter, but we couldn't.

After just eight days, someone decided that Lobo was miraculously healed of his worms. We made plans to take him to his exhibit in the main zoo. We leashed him, and he sat with his keeper in the back of a pick-up truck. He was so excited, he wagged his tail wildly and licked everyone within licking distance. I think he knew where he was going and was showing his appreciation.

When we arrived, there was Missy in her elegant gray glory, looking feminine. Her eyes adored Lobo; her body trembled with excitement. Lobo leapt off the truck bed and dragged his keeper to the cage. Missy stepped back, and Lobo was released into her care.

Both wolves observed wolf etiquette: Missy stood in one place, but not still, while Lobo walked around her, sniffing her to make a memory. Once that was accomplished, they played. Wolves play tag, wrestle, fight, race, and then they rest. Lobo lay back exhausted, and Missy laid her head across his neck. It was plain to see that they were in wolf heaven. A bond was formed, and they would stay together for life.

Lobo formed another bond—a bond with his keeper, Al Bristacoff. Lobo was easy to love, and Al was proud of this new addition to his string of animals. It was evident that Lobo loved Al; whenever Al got to work, Lobo was at the cage door whining for attention. Al set aside time daily to play with Lobo, and playing with humans was something Lobo had known since birth. They were an intriguing matchup because Al was short. When Lobo jumped up and placed his feet on Al's shoulders, he stood taller than Al. He was also 65 pounds heavier than Al.

Though Lobo acted more like a dog than a wolf, Missy showed him the wolf ropes. She liked people too, but she was not nearly as enthusiastic around them as Lobo. Lobo loved to be petted by the keepers and would lean against the wire at the front of his cage hoping people would lean over the rail to pet him. They often did.

A year and a half after Lobo's arrival at the zoo, he sealed his bond with Missy and she began to carry his puppies. A whelping box was installed at the back of the exhibit so that Missy would have a warm, dry spot to have her first litter. She instinctively began to spend more time in her den, and Lobo, not liking to be separated from her, stayed in the den as well. For weeks the public couldn't get a look at these two special animals as they prepared to become proud parents.

The night of delivery came right on schedule, and five wolf pups, healthy and strong, were born to Missy and Lobo. Lobo was in the den, supervising the process and showing tender care to his beloved mate. He licked the new pups, leaving them clean and shiny, and then lay close to them so that they might borrow his body heat. He stayed in the whelping box for several days to help with the young. When Missy needed to rest from the pups and stretch and eat, Lobo would stay behind. He did everything but nurse the pups. He was an excellent husband and father and in every way continued to win the respect of the zoo staff who knew him.

Lobo became more special to us when the pups came out of the den. He was obviously proud of his family and more in love with Missy than ever. Lobo was always careful not to step on his pups, who were forever attacking his legs and awkwardly falling in front of him. When he lay down, they tugged his ears, pulled on the hair around his muzzle, and relentlessly harassed him—but to no avail. In fact, he just glowed as we watched, he was so proud of each of them.

Al was allowed all the privileges of a favorite uncle. Neither Lobo nor Missy was at all disturbed by his presence. He could and did play with the pups all the time. Lobo just watched, with no reaction except a wag of his tail, which of course was a sign of approval.

When the pups were six weeks old, it was decided that Gib Brush, the zoo photographer, would take a family portrait. He and his assistant came down to the yard. For the first time, Lobo and Missy seemed agitated. They paced back and forth, occasionally running to the gate to stare at the photographers assembling their equipment. The stares were intense and ominous, but no one took them seriously because Lobo and Missy had only received and given affection for 20 months.

Finally Gib and his assistant were ready for the session, and Al led them into the cage. Al went in first, then Gib and his helper. The puppies, now almost seven weeks old, were playing as usual, and Lobo stood in front of them and stared at Gib. Al noticed that Lobo's hair was on end, and he moved over to pet him and calm him down. Lobo kept an eye on Gib and relaxed for the moment.

Gib kept moving around to get an angle. It's hard to say, but I believe Lobo was interpreting Gib's movements as a sign that he was looking for an opportunity to hurt the puppies.

Lobo suddenly exploded with a ferocious growl and bark. He charged Gib viciously, grabbed Gib's leg below the knee, and clamped down with his now massive jaws. Everyone was in shock when they heard Gib's leg crack. Al grabbed Lobo and pulled him off and asked Gib's assistant to help Gib out of the cage immediately. Gib was pale and in danger of going into shock. He was an older man and suffering from the early stages of lung cancer. Once Gib was out of the cage, Lobo calmed down, even taking the time to lick Al's hand.

Gib was rushed to the local hospital, where X-rays confirmed what was already known: his leg was severely fractured. He would wear a cast for a few months. From that day on, it was clear that Lobo was not safe for everyone, though he was safe for most. There was no apparent reason for his discrimination of some people, unless his sense of smell was telling him something we could not discern. He was never aggressive with any of the veterinarians, but he would growl at civilians, so to speak. He would also occasionally pick people out of crowds and watch them guardedly. He was like his father, good for most but not for all.

Lobo was a magnificent animal. His luxuriant coat always shone in the morning sun. He was massive and strong. His eyes were expressive and clear; his face full of character. Missy was pretty, but next to Lobo she was average. Of course, he didn't think so. To him, Missy was Miss Canada, and, in the manner of wolves, he loved her for a lifetime.

One June morning, a young couple decided that their four-year-old should see the zoo. They were animal lovers, and it had been five years since they had gone to the zoo themselves. They arrived at 10:00 A.M. and walked right in. They promised their little girl that they would visit the children's zoo just before they went home, saying, "If you're a good little girl in the main zoo, you can feed and pet the animals at the children's zoo just before we leave."

They enjoyed the aquatics section, especially the sea lions and polar bears. The sea lions were always entertaining, but the polar bears were drawing the crowds this particular Saturday. Polaris, the male, dove headfirst into his pool from a four-foot ledge. We could tell he was enjoying himself and the crowd's reaction. He wouldn't stay in the pool long, climbing out only to run and dive into the pool again. The four-year-old daughter was screaming with delight and laughing exuberantly with each of the polar bear's dives.

The small family stopped at the snack stand for soft drinks and popcorn, and then headed for the North American section. There they visited the coyotes, raccoons, wolverines, badgers, arctic foxes, and Canadian lynx.

The parents looked at each other briefly when they saw that the next exhibit housed the wolves. It had been nearly five years since Niki had run away, but the memory of it was still painful. Their first moments at the exhibit turned out not to be painful at all; in fact it was pleasurable, even heartwarming. Lobo and Missy were on their third litter of pups, and the whole wolf family was involved in an all-out romp. As usual, Lobo was allowing himself to get the worst of it.

One aggressive little female actually hung from his ear when he lifted his head. The crowd laughed and the young family with them.

Lobo hadn't been paying much attention to the crowd, but one young woman's laugh caught his attention. Something deep within him was stirred, and vague and warm memories surfaced. He knew that voice! It was an echo from his past. He searched the crowd and stopped when he saw the couple. He looked from one to the other and began to remember car rides, being held, chasing balls, and especially digging. He missed digging; his cage floor was cement. He noticed that the couple now had a little puppy of their own. He began to wag his tail and whined a greeting to them.

They were, of course, amazed that this magnificent wolf was paying attention to them. The husband turned to his wife and asked, "You don't think for a minute that . . ." Anticipating his question, she said, "Oh, come on. Niki could never have gotten that big. We just must have a way with wolves or . . ."

Lobo continued to greet them and just them, while a dozen other people looked on. He was carrying on, whining and wagging his tail with unmistakable enthusiasm.

The young mother stared in disbelief and said, "Niki?"

Lobo leaned against the wire to be petted and looked over his shoulder in a loving and friendly way. She bent over the rail and scratched his back through the wire. He licked her fingers, and she knew in her heart that this was Niki.

After Lobo finished greeting them, he returned to his beloved Missy and lay next to her. He kissed her enthusiastically and looked back at the couple as if to say, "Hey, look what I found!"

Al Bristacoff, who normally avoided the public if possible, coincidentally walked by while the couple was there. The wife stepped up to him and asked, "Are you the keeper for these animals?"

Al nodded and asked if he could answer any questions.

She asked, "Could you tell me how the zoo got that male wolf?"

Al looked at her for a moment and wondered why she had singled out the male for that question. Then he shrugged and answered, "About five years ago the animal shelter in Pasadena asked if someone could come down and tell them whether or not they had picked up a wolf. As you can see they had.

"We brought him back to the zoo, and he's been here ever since. He was about six months old, I think, when he came, and had a red collar. Evidently he was somebody's pet that got away. People who try to keep wolves as pets are nuts. A wolf gets dangerous. Lobo himself has changed. He used to like everybody, but now just a few people can be sure that he won't attack them. Not too long ago, he bit the zoo photographer and broke his leg. Why do you ask?"

The young mother didn't want to be one of the nuts who would keep a wolf, so she just said, "He was so friendly. I just wondered."

Her husband squeezed her hand, affirming her choice not to admit that they were the nuts who had raised Niki as a pet. They thanked Al for talking with them and stayed to enjoy a last moment with an old friend.

Lobo was playing with his pups, and Missy was looking on proudly.

"He's better off. It worked out for the best, didn't it?" said the husband. "Our yard looks nice, and our dog Skippy wouldn't hurt anybody. We got to have Niki when he was safe and loving. We had him when it was best for us, and the zoo got him when it was best for them. Doesn't he look happy?"

She squeezed her husband's hand and nodded.

They watched the wolves until their little girl got impatient and said, "I want to go pet the animals in the children's zoo." They left with old questions answered. They left with the knowledge that things had worked out for the best.

• • •

I have now lived long enough to believe that Romans 8:28 is 100 percent true: "We know that in everything God works for good with those who love him, who are called according to his purpose." That means no matter how dark our circumstances are today, they will work out. Every one of our lives is an autobiography in process. We may be in a sad or devastating chapter right now, but we are assured that—because of Jesus—the final chapter has already been written and has a happy ending. As Romans 8:37-39 says,

> In all these things we are more than conquerors through him who loved us. For I am sure that neither death, nor life, nor angels, nor principalities, nor powers, nor things present, nor things to come, nor height, nor depth, nor anything else in all creation, will be able to separate us from the love of God in Christ Jesus our Lord.

CHAPTER FIFTEEN

The Intervention

I couldn't say I hadn't been warned. I had been . . . and by the most respected keeper at the zoo. He had walked right up to me two months before and said, "Richmond, did anybody tell you about the kudu?" (A kudu is an extremely large, 600-pound antelope with horns that spiral 36 inches above its head. It is tan and white with soft vertical stripes on its muscular sides. The females are more delicate and have no horns.)

"No, Jack," I responded. "Is there something I should know?"

"Be careful," he said matter-of-factly. Then he walked back to his section.

No one knew more about African hoofstock than Jack Badal. He had been given the Marlin Perkins Award for his amazing accomplishments with hoofstock. So if he said I should be careful, then careful I would be.

I did a little research and discovered that the male kudu becomes sexually mature at two years. Our male had just reached that milestone. Smaller 60-pound antelopes can become a bit dangerous during breeding season, but a 600-pound greater kudu could be lethal. Even lions avoided such an animal.

I began to watch and noticed some subtle changes. First, the kudu began to withdraw from human contact. Then he took to sharpening his horns on the granite walls of his compound. I watched him carefully, knowing of his potential.

When I worked this section I would arrive at the zoo at 4:45 A.M. and check my animals. If anything happened during the night, I wanted to be the one who discovered it. If everything checked out, I would spend the next hour reading at the golf course clubhouse adjacent to the zoo, then begin my 6:00 A.M. to 2:30 P.M. schedule.

I'll never forget a June morning in 1968. It was an hour before sunrise and very foggy. The zoo is eerie when it's dark and downright scary when the fog is draping the streetlights and muffling the sounds. I walked by the impala and noticed that they were standing with their ears cocked toward the kudu barn. Henry, the saddle-bill stork, was pacing. Normally he would be on one leg asleep. Something was up! I hurried my pace.

When I reached the kudus, my heart was gripped with terror. The male was viciously attacking the females. Unless I was successful in separating them, the females would be killed. I knew what was happening. In the wild the females would be giving off a scent that attracts and provokes the males. The males would fight each other for days; and when the strongest emerged, they would claim the females and mating would begin. In a zoo there are no extra males to fight and the females are not ready to mate. The male becomes enraged when the females reject him and they become the recipients of his wrath.

At the time, the kudus were in their night quarters, a small 40-by-40-foot corral adjacent to where they were put on public display during the day. It was the largest yard in the zoo. I thought the females might live if I was successful in letting them out so they could avoid him. The problem was that in order to let them out, I had to enter and walk completely across the small corral. The male didn't look as if he wanted company, but something had to be done now.

I grabbed a rake and shovel and placed them in a wheelbarrow. I unlocked the gate and stepped into the corral. Everything became still . . . and it seemed as if I had entered a bad dream. The male stared at me and shook his head in challenge. I whistled "Amazing Grace" and began to back across the corral. He stalked me like a cat stalks a mouse. His eyes were full of rage. I finally reached the other side and fumbled for the lock. I turned the key, keeping one eye on the enraged male, who was standing 15 feet in front of me. The lock clicked and I slid it out of the hasp. The male charged. I could see the finely sharpened tips of his horns headed for my chest. I threw myself against the gate. It gave way and I fell backwards. There was a brown blur, a sickening thud, and a mournful cry. A female had run for the gate and taken my blow. I scrambled up the chain-link gate and cast myself out of the exhibit. I landed on my back seven feet below on a thick bed of ivy where, for several seconds, I pondered the question, *Am I alive?* My heart was pounding and I was soaking wet. I took those to be good signs.

After 30 minutes of intense efforts, I was able to separate the male from the females. He was locked in a barn for two weeks and let out when the females were ready for him. Both females gave birth several months later. One of them always wore a scar where the male gored her when he attempted to kill me. Her saving my life had not been intentional, but I always gave her special treatment after that. I loved her for what she had done.

After that incident, it occurred to me that this was not the first time someone else had taken punishment for me. It had happened before, only on that occasion my Savior had known exactly what He was doing and what it would mean. His death on the cross was no accident; that was God's plan all along. Jesus willingly left His place of glory and authority in heaven to live among a people who treated Him like anything but a King. And He never wavered from His purpose—to die and take a punishment He didn't deserve. As Isaiah 53:5 says,

> He was pierced through for our transgressions, He was crushed for our iniquities; the chastening for our well-being fell upon Him, and by His scourging we are healed.

Have you thanked Jesus lately? Perhaps it's time you did.

CHAPTER SIXTEEN

The Black Widow

One of the greatest lessons I have learned from the animal kingdom was not learned at the zoo. It was learned in a mossy, moldy greenhouse in the backyard of a lady who I was sure was a witch.

Spring was just giving way to summer. School was almost out, and like all eight-year-old boys I was looking forward to three months of no shoes, except on Sunday, and a creative string of adventures yet to be lived out. My mother was just beginning to fix dinner when the afternoon stillness was broken by the persistent ring of the front doorbell. At the door stood an older man. His tie was loosened and he was drenched with perspiration. He wiped the sweat from his forehead and began his to-the-point presentation, one that he had probably given 50 times before coming to our front door.

"Hello, Ma'am. My name is Edgar Beasly and I'm from the health department. We are going door-to-door to alert people that they need to spray for black widow spiders. I bet you have already noticed that there are more spiders than usual this year. Doctors are reporting many bites that they feel are probably black widow bites. Last week a little girl nearly died from one. So we're here to warn you that we are having an epidemic of black widow spiders in California. This sometimes happens after a wet spring."

He handed my mother a little book and said, "Ma'am, here's a pamphlet that gives you some important information about black widows. It shows you what they look like, and more importantly, what their webs look like. We'd sure be much obliged if you'd spray."

When Mr. Beasly left, my mother scanned the pamphlet. She looked at me with legitimate concern and said, "Gary, if I ever catch you so much as walking by a black widow spider web, I'll spank your back side shiny. Do you understand me, young man?"

I nodded that I did and she handed me the pamphlet. I was fascinated. On the cover was a menacing picture of a female black widow. She looked large and was posed so that she revealed the red hourglass on the underside of her shiny black abdomen. The pamphlet made note that she lived in an irregular web that would likely be found in dark places like garages, wood piles, and under cabinets.

The section that most caught my interest was entitled, "The Bite of the Black Widow Spider." It said that a person who was bitten might experience the following symptoms: discoloration at the site of the bite, nausea, a severe headache, unusual swelling, labored breathing, and blurred vision. It said that some children even died from the bite of the black widow spider.

My mother never realized that she had just provided a road map for my next great adventure, a black widow safari. I couldn't wait to tell my best friend, Doug, about the greatest idea of my life.

"Now here it is, Doug. On Saturday morning my parents will be gone for three hours. I figure that will give us time to catch ten black widow spiders. We can take those bandits down to Eliot Junior High School and dump them on this red ant hill that I found. It will be great. The red ants will come streaming out to protect their home and there will be a scary fight. The red ants will win and we will have done our part in Altadena's battle to fight the black widows."

"What if we get bit?" Doug asked.

"We're not going to let those child-killers get us. We'll be real careful. Hey, you're not going to chicken out on me, are you?"

"Well, no," Doug added defensively.

I made Doug perform the blood-brother handshake and promise not to tell any living soul what we were going to do at 8:30 Saturday morning. He took the oath, knowing that if he broke it his teeth and hair would fall out. I found an old peanut butter jar and poked a few holes in the lid. We didn't want any of the spiders dying before they got a chance to fight the red ants. We chose a two-foot stick for catching the spiders, and then we hid our safari gear behind the garage until Saturday.

As soon as my parents left to go shopping, I ran to Doug's house. He was already waiting for me in his front yard. We grabbed our gear and headed for my backyard. I had already located several webs. On the way there we ran into another good friend, Eric, who was coming over to see if we could play. We finally decided that we'd better let him in, but we made him take an even more solemn oath than Doug had taken.

"What kind of oath?" asked Eric.

"The kind that, if you break it, something scary happens."

Eric really wanted in, so he took the oath.

"I, Eric . . ."

"I, Eric . . ."

". . . promise never to tell about the black widow safari."

". . . promise never to tell about the black widow safari."

"If I do, my mother's hair will fall out."

"What?"

"You heard me, Eric. Do you want in or not?"

"It's just that I don't want my mom's hair to fall out."

"Are you planning to tell someone?"

"No . . ."

"Then you don't have anything to worry about. There's a reason for this, Eric. You're not good at keeping secrets and this will help you."

"Okay," said Eric. "If I do, my mother's hair will fall out."

"That wasn't so bad, was it?" asked Doug.

We walked down our long overgrown driveway and ran right into my 12-year-old brother, Steve. Before we could stop him, Eric blurted out, "Guess what, Steve? We're going to catch ten black widow spiders and dump them on a red ant hill. Isn't that neat?"

My brother then treated us to the words we least liked to hear. "You guys are too young!"

Boy, I hated those words. Steve told us we were too little to catch black widow spiders, but agreed it sounded like a great idea. He offered to catch the spiders for us, and if we were good he would let us hold the jar.

As we followed my brother to our backyard, I held up my fist to Eric and said, "I'm never going to tell you a secret again. I hope you're thinking about what you just did to your mother, you oathbreaker."

I sadly handed over the catching stick to my brother and Doug reluctantly handed the peanut butter jar to me. Eric was trying to visualize his mother bald and wondering if she would know that it was his fault.

It took only a minute to find the first spider. She was residing behind our tool shed. Her web was spun between the fence and the shed and bore the evidence of many a successful hunt. The dried bodies of three moths and two flies were mute reminders of her deadly capacities.

We crowded behind Steve to watch him catch the first of the ten spiders. He managed to get her on the end of the stick and called for me to open the jar. With trembling hands I opened the jar, and with a tap of the stick it received its first prisoner. She was medium sized and looked none too happy about being caught. She looked just like the spider on the pamphlet, and when I lifted the jar we were able to see the bright red hourglass on her shiny black abdomen.

As the jar began to fill up, my job became more and more difficult. The fifth spider attached a web to the lid so that when I opened the jar for the sixth spider I pulled the fifth across my hand.

After we had caught eight spiders we faced a dilemma. We ran out of spiders to catch on our property. Steve wanted to stop at eight, but I insisted that since we had agreed to catch ten that was exactly the number we should catch. Steve gave in, but he had no idea as to where we should hunt next. Eric, who had been the quiet observer on the safari, made a great suggestion. "I bet the evil queen of the black widow spiders lives in Mrs. Brown's greenhouse." Mrs. Brown lived next door to Doug, and all the neighborhood children were afraid of her. She hated small children and would call the police on them if they even set foot on her property. Some of us were convinced that she was a witch and could cast spells that could keep us under her power and things like that.

What made Eric's idea so attractive was that catching the spiders had become too easy, and besides, my brother Steve was having all the fun. It was such a great idea that Eric was forgiven for breaking the oath and we told him so.

He said he was glad because he couldn't get used to the idea of having a bald mother. He said he thought it might be embarrassing.

Doug suggested that we sneak onto Mrs. Brown's property from his backyard. Her greenhouse was at the very end of her backyard, so Doug's suggestion made sense. We peered over Doug's fence into the untrimmed jungle that made up her yard and concluded that she was not outside.

One at a time we dropped into forbidden territory and slipped silently into the greenhouse.

It was damp and dark, musty and moldy—perfect for black widows. We all felt that Mrs. Brown would jump out and grab us at any minute, so we asked Eric to keep watch.

Underneath Mrs. Brown's gardening bench was a five-gallon red clay pot. It was the kind my mother used to pot a small palm tree. It was turned upside down and resting on three red bricks. Steve and Doug turned it over slowly and carefully. We each drew in our breath at what we saw. At the bottom of that clay pot was the largest black widow we had ever seen. She was fat and seemed to be throbbing with poison. She was protecting her silky white egg sac, and unlike the other spiders, she was simply not afraid of the stick.

After considerable effort, Steve was able to get the deadly giant on the end of the stick. He called for me to open the jar. I shook the jar until I was able to count the eight spiders we had already captured. Carefully, I turned the lid and removed it from the jar. I stood there with trembling hands while Steve brought the stick to the mouth of the jar. Just at the moment he was going to tap her into the jar, she made a jump for it. She landed right between my bare feet. I backed away, and in the excitement I forgot to put the lid back on the jar. My full attention was directed to the escapee between my feet, and I watched with rapt attention as my brother struggled to get her back on the stick.

I failed to notice that a medium-sized female was crawling out of the jar and onto the back of my hand. Slowly, I became aware of an eerie sensation and stared in disbelief at the little killer that was taking a morning stroll on my hand. I let the jar slip through my fingers, and black widows began to run everywhere. They mattered little anymore. The game was over. I was unable to speak words that had meaning but I managed a pretty good sound. I believe that phonetically it sounded a little like "YaaaaaaAAAAAAAAAA!" My brother looked at me and it was clear that he was experiencing fear also.

Now I believe that our fear was of different natures. The fear that I was experiencing was because for the first time in my life I really believed that I was going to die. Not like in Cowboys and Indians where you could get up again, but the sort of death where everything goes dark, and after that I wasn't sure what would happen. It took all my strength to keep from fainting. I could feel every footfall of the spider on the back of my hand. I stayed perfectly still.

I begged my brother with my tear-filled eyes to please get the spider off my hand. He moved his index finger into a flicking position and placed it within an inch of the spider. I held my breath and wanted to close my eyes, but I was afraid that if I did it would be for the last time. The spider stopped as if to consider what threat the finger was going to pose, and when she did, Steve flicked with all his might. The spider went flying. I have never felt a greater sense of relief in my life. Neither have I before or since learned a more important truth: Someday I am going to die.

How you feel about that truth has everything to do with how you prepare for it. If you have no belief in God or a future existence, then it really doesn't matter how you live your life. On the other hand, if you do believe in God, then everything you do matters. The Bible has two verses that greatly intrigue me:

> It is appointed for men to die once, and after that comes judgment (Hebrews 9:27).

We were designed to live for eternity. But because of sin, we have an appointment with death and nothing we can do will make us early or late. Read what James had to say concerning life and death:

> Come now, you who say, "Today or tomorrow, we shall go to such and such a city, and spend a year there and engage in business and make a

> profit." Yet you do not know what your life will be like tomorrow. You are just a vapor that appears for a little while and then vanishes away. Instead, you ought to say, "If the Lord wills, we shall live and also do this or that" (James 4:13-15 NASB).

Scripture clearly teaches that there is a God, and what we do matters a great deal to Him. It is also clear that whatever we're going to accomplish needs to be accomplished before we die.

The wisest man who ever lived wrote a dissertation on his search for truth and wisdom. His final words and conclusions are as follows:

> The end of the matter; all has been heard. Fear God and keep His commandments; for this is the whole duty of man. For God will bring every deed into judgment, with every secret thing, whether good or evil (Ecclesiastes 12:13-14).

It is a startling revelation to know that the whole of our lives will be lived between two great pillars—both of which will be noted on our gravestones—our birthdate is one pillar, and our obituary the other. Anything of value that you accomplish will exist between those two pillars. Not knowing the day of our death heightens the value of each day that we have to live.

It would be wise to consider the implications of this closing thought:

> See that ye walk circumspectly, not as fools, but as wise, redeeming the time, because the days are evil (Ephesians 5:16 KJV).

Chapter Seventeen

The Mayor Is Coming

During my years at the zoo, I came to dread the announcement, "The mayor is coming." It wasn't that we were going to meet him. That would have been fun. Instead, it meant that we had to clean up the zoo in places where we didn't know we had places. We had to transform the zoo into an immaculate display for the mayor to see.

I remember once being made to clean up some building material behind an obscure barn in an obscure corner of the zoo. I offered my opinion that I didn't think the mayor would be coming behind this barn. The restroom facilities in the main zoo were perfectly acceptable.

My supervisor smiled. "Richmond," he said, "I'm paid to think. You are paid to do."

He must have been telling the truth, I thought, because I had never seen him do anything. I told him I didn't know what kind of money he made, but it must be a thrill to be so overpaid for his responsibility. He smiled again and pointed to the back of the barn and motioned for me to start working.

So all around the zoo, we shoveled and hosed and scrubbed and scoured until each section virtually gleamed with purity. And then we waited. And waited. And waited. Finally, the zoo closed for the day and we all went home exhausted and a little irritated.

But that is how it was. I can recall at least ten occasions when the mayor was announced and he never came. He did come to the front of the zoo one day, however, to have his picture taken with 15 children from the Taiwanese community, who were bused in for a public-relations shot. He gave a little speech about how he had been personally responsible for this marvelous zoo and then he kissed a child, sustaining the kiss until all the media flashbulbs had burnt themselves to smithereens. Then he walked away, completely unaware of the enormous manpower exerted on his behalf.

I inquired as to the possible reasons why he never actually came into the zoo, and was informed that he once had. Amazed, I asked what miracle had attracted him. Mark, one of our zoo's leading humorists, offered, "He must have caught the scent of cameras."

"It's the truth," offered another keeper. "He came to see the white rhinos, Sonny and Cher, let out for the first time. He made everybody wait until he arrived. When he got there he spent ten minutes looking for a place to stand where the television cameras would be sure to capture him when the rhinos made their first entrance. The mayor and his entourage climbed through wild roses and ankle-deep ivy to stand on the hill just behind the exhibit. It turned out to be, as expected, the very best view for television. The mayor signaled the keeper to let the white rhinos out and filming began. Sonny snorted and pranced out in a thunderous manner, followed by his saucy mate. The crowd cheered and, as if trained, the rhinos stopped to consider their public right below the mayor. He couldn't have planned it better. But he did leave one important consideration to chance."

"What was that?" I asked in rapt attention.

"The automatic sprinklers," said the keeper, beginning to laugh hysterically. "They came on with a vengeance. The television news teams got it all. There were dignitaries running in every direction. They were soaked. It was great!"

"What did the mayor do?" I asked.

"He just left. I heard he was really bent out of shape. Anyway, I think that's why he doesn't come into the zoo anymore. He's probably still mad."

That story sort of made up for all the extra work we had to do, I thought.

In fairness, it occurred to me that perhaps we dreaded the mayor's "visits" because of the extra work. We might even have looked forward to his coming if we hadn't let things get so far behind. We shouldn't have let junk accumulate; there was no reason for it.

• • •

There is another visitor who is coming, and we've had plenty of advance notice to prepare for Him. I'm sure you know that I am referring to the return of the Lord Jesus Christ. Of course, we have no idea *when* He is coming; all we know is that He will come unexpectedly, "like a thief in the night" (1 Thessalonians 5:2). Like a concerned Army general, He will inspect us with an absolutely thorough review. Over and over the Bible cautions us to be ready, to prepare for His coming.

The apostle Paul eagerly anticipated our Lord's return. He wrote,

> There is laid up for me the crown of righteousness, which the Lord, the righteous judge, will award to me on that Day, and not only to me but also to all who have loved his appearing (2 Timothy 4:8).

The phrase "loved his appearing" has always intrigued me. That refers to those who are ready and current in their walk with Jesus. The folks who have let a lot of waste material accumulate in their lives would dread the thought of His coming.

How about you? Are you up to date? Or do you have some serious cleaning to do in your life?

Chapter Eighteen

Perpetual Adolescents

There are two kinds of chimpanzees: those that let things happen and those that make things happen. Our zoo had both, and they both caused a pile of trouble.

Zoo chimps are bored. They really don't have enough to do and it makes them a little crazy most of the time.

Much of their time is spent waiting. They wait to be let out in the morning. They wait for enough food to get them through the day. They wait to be let in at night so that they can eat their fill and sleep till morning. They watch people watching them and sometimes they throw things at the people (disgusting things). They fight a little and play a little, but mostly they wait.

So it's not surprising that the day they were offered an opportunity for diversion they took it. You see, one of the zoo patrons noticed that there was a 50-foot long, one-inch hose neatly coiled right in front of the chimp exhibit.

He must have said to himself, "Self, if you throw that hose over the edge of the exhibit, it will provide an excellent escape ladder for the chimps." And that is exactly what he did.

He couldn't have realized the dangerous situation that he was creating for the public. Most of our chimps were neurotic, and when they were out of the exhibit they could become quite excited. The adults were four to six times as strong as a man, and a good number of them had periods during which they were very aggressive for no apparent reason.

While the chimps were making their escape, I was counting the minutes until quitting time. That was not my usual practice, but then this was not a usual day. It was June 19 and it was my seventh wedding anniversary. My wife, Carol, would be looking good and my mouth was watering for prime rib. When the phone rang, I felt a twinge of fear that something was going to make me late for our celebration.

I couldn't have been more accurate. A security guard calmly informed us that eight chimpanzees were out of their moated area and mingling with the public. We grabbed our capture equipment and headed out.

When we arrived we were treated to one of the more frightening sights I have ever witnessed. Jeanie, a highly unpredictable and sometimes aggressive female, was hovering over a baby stroller. Her mouth was wide open and her lethal teeth were resting against the skull of a three-month-old baby girl. Jeanie was not showing any signs of aggression, but that didn't mean that two seconds later she wouldn't be. The baby's mother looked concerned, but she didn't appear to be unduly frightened. I cautioned our new vet not to make any moves until Jeanie was clear of the baby.

Some of the other chimps noticed me because I was in uniform, and they began to holler. Jeanie looked around, saw us, and took off running. All of the chimps knew we had a tranquilizer gun, and they began to back away. I called out to the zoo patrons that these chimps were dangerous and told them to leave the area for their own safety. We wouldn't attempt any capture activity until the people were safely out of sight.

When we finally exposed the tranquilizer gun, a very funny thing happened. Toto, our oldest and largest male, led three of the females back to the hose and climbed back into the exhibit. This group huddled together and patted each other. That's what chimps do to comfort each other when they are upset.

Other keepers began to arrive, and two of the babies recognized them and crawled into their arms. They had sensed the fear in their parents and were in an emotional turmoil. But they calmed down quickly when the keepers carried them to the back of their exhibit.

Only two chimps rebelled—the erratic Jeanie and the delicate Antoinette, more affectionately known as Annie. They climbed a guardrail and made their way deep into the landscaping between their own moat and the Indian rhino yard. Herman, the Indian rhino, was beside himself with rage. He charged and snorted and even reared up slightly, hoping to get a chance to bash a chimp.

The growth between the two exhibits made the capture work more difficult because it was a dense, non-negotiable tangle of wild roses and ivy. Our job was to get into a position where we could shoot a tranquilizer dart into Jeanie first in the hopes that Annie would surrender and climb back into the moat. Dr. Bradford felt that since he was paid the most, he should take the risk of shooting the angry chimp. I told him I thought he was right. He carried the rifle over the guardrail and I followed him with a backup pistol in case the first shot missed. We spread the wild roses apart and saw our two escapees. They were huddled in the shadows and screamed their disapproval at our presence.

Dr. Bradford took careful aim and a blast of air propelled a dart swiftly to Jeanie's generous hindquarters. She reacted instantly, but not the way we had hoped. She charged at us screaming with anger, her teeth showing from ear to ear.

I knew that as soon as she saw my pistol she would stop and run away, but Dr. Bradford didn't know that, so he made a run for it. He was a big man, and when he turned to run he knocked me flat. The pistol went flying. Dr. Bradford tripped over me and began to fall into the rhino moat. Herman, more enraged than ever, was trying his best to horn the doctor. As Dr. Bradford was falling I had grabbed one leg and was now holding on to him for dear life. I was sure Jeanie was going to bite us any second so I had closed my eyes to concentrate on keeping the vet out of the rhino yard. She must have seen the pistol before it went flying and ceased her charge because we were never bitten.

With great effort, the doctor pulled himself back over the edge of the moat and breathlessly thanked me for grabbing him. We peered back into the undergrowth and saw Jeanie showing the effects of the powerful tranquilizer. As we had hoped, Annie jumped back into the exhibit by herself. And three minutes later, Jeanie was asleep for the night.

Chimpanzees are perpetual adolescents, never quite ready to take responsibility for the freedom they so desperately seem to want. Of all the great apes, they are the most playful and the least dignified. They are childlike. At the time of this writing, Toto is nearly 50 years of age and still totally irresponsible. In fact, from what I could gather, he is worse than ever. But it's okay because Toto is a chimp.

• • •

One of the fundamental differences between a man and a chimpanzee is that a man may choose to become responsible. If we are responsible, we have opted for maturity. We have grown up. If we are possessed of all our faculties, growing up is what we are supposed to do. It is expected of us, and if we don't, other people, usually our parents, are disappointed and embarrassed.

The apostle Paul was disappointed with the church members in the city of Corinth. They never grew up. His words express how he felt:

> I, brethren, could not address you as spiritual men, but as men of the flesh, as babes in Christ. I fed you with milk, not solid food; for you were not ready for it; and even yet you are not ready, for you are still of the flesh. For while there is jealousy and strife among you, are you not of the flesh, and behaving like ordinary men (1 Corinthians 3:1-3)?

It's not that the Corinthian Christians didn't have the knowledge that adults acquire, because they did. It's not that they didn't have the Spirit of God, because they did. They were babies because they couldn't take the responsibility for the freedom to serve and obey Christ. They wouldn't care for others. Like children and adolescents they simply focused on their own needs. But people who are mature in Christ focus on the needs of other people.

The author of Hebrews shares his thoughts about maturity. He says,

> About this we have much to say which is hard to explain, since you have become dull of hearing. For though by this time you ought to be teachers, you need some one to teach you again the first principles of God's word. You need milk, not solid food; for every one who lives on milk is unskilled in the word of righteousness, for he is a child. But solid food is for the mature, for those who have their faculties trained by practice to distinguish good from evil (Hebrews 5:11-14).

How can we know if we're moving toward maturity? Would you please consider with me these three questions?

1. On whose needs are you focused?

2. Are you consistent in doing the right things?

3. Are you serving others?

We could never say to a chimp, "Isn't it time to grow up?" But it is a question we may want to ask ourselves. From my own personal experience, there are some people who need to be told to grow up. I can say that with authority because there was a time in my life when someone came to me and said, "Richmond, grow up!" I was hurt at the time, but made the changes that were suggested because I knew even at that time they were for my own good. What God said in Proverbs 27:6 was true: "Faithful are the wounds of a friend."

My hope is that you were able to respond to the above three questions with these answers: 1) others; 2) yes; 3) yes. If not, then now is a good time to take a step in the right direction. Can you think of a need or two in the life of another person? What can you do today or this week to meet that need? Whatever you decide to do, let it be done without any thought of getting something in return.

And from here onward, remember to practice what you learn about the Christian life at the time you learn it. In no time at all, you will be maturing nicely.

Chapter Nineteen

Love Stories

Have you ever wondered if animals have the capacity for love? I have been asked dozens of times, and to me the answer is a resounding yes! It's all too evident. Some people, though, are skeptical and want some kind of proof. So without shame I offer it to you.

First, let's define love to ensure that we are on the same wavelength. Sometime ago I read C. S. Lewis's book *The Four Loves,* and it was one of the most enlightening experiences of my life. Lewis outlined four kinds of love, each distinct and different from the other. First, he said that there were loves and likings for the subhuman: love for country, the way you feel when you hear the national anthem played, apple pie, your pet, Christmas music, your hometown, an old sweatshirt.

Second, Lewis said that all of us have affections. These have no rational explanations. We are just drawn to them for no good reason. He called this mother love. For example, I was told as a child that I was the kind of person that only a mother could love. At the time those words sailed right over my head. Now I understand them because I have met children who are a lot like I was. Affection makes it possible for you to tolerate your child's behavior in a restaurant when others would prefer not to.

Friendship was the third love discussed by C. S. Lewis. He said that the foundation for friendship is a store of things in common. He quoted William Wordsworth: "Friends are those who see the same truth." I guarantee you that your closest friends are those with whom you have the most in common.

In discussing the last level of human love, Lewis points out that numbers are significant. Two's company and three's a crowd. That love, of course, is romance. The idea of romance is to become one with a beloved. Lewis mentioned that in friendship we see two friends looking to the horizon, but in romance we see two lovers looking into each other's eyes. Love's kiss is different, too. Kissing Mom good-bye is special, but it differs a great deal from a lover's passionate kiss in the moonlight.

These are the human loves: likings, affection, friendship, and romance. Each love is unique and easily identified, and they are wonderful inventions of God that we enjoy all of our lives. Without love, life wouldn't even be worth living.

Let's get back now to our first question: Do animals have the capacity for love? More specifically, do they have loves like those described by C. S. Lewis? Let me share with you what I saw at the zoo, and I'll let you come to your own conclusion. Because we think of animals as subhuman, you might call their equivalent love something like "loves and likings of the subanimal." I saw this love all the time when I worked at the zoo; but it was never more apparent than when Eloise, a three-year-old orangutan, came for a month's stay at the health center.

Eloise had an undiagnosed rash over most of her body. She was as miserable as any patient I have ever seen, animal or human. Her illness turned out to be a type of herpes that would be with her from time to time for the rest of her life.

She itched more than anyone can imagine. Of course, scratching just caused more itching. She cried as she scratched and sometimes threw herself against the side of her cage and rubbed her body against it, hoping that her itching would stop.

The veterinarians used drugs to alleviate her itching, but almost everything they gave her seemed useless. Only sleep-inducing drugs brought any relief to Eloise. Unfortunately, they couldn't just keep sedating her; that only created a new set of problems.

Eloise needed comfort, but because the herpes virus was very communicable, we were not able to offer much aid. Some of the staff would put on rubber gloves and simply sit and hold her hand, or they would reach into her cage and rub her back and arms with benadryl or cortisone cream. She would look at us with very loving eyes that pled for more help than we were able to give. There was, however, one remedy that helped more than anything: Eloise had to have her security blanket. She was lost without it. Actually, it was only a bath towel. Fortunately it was a white bath towel, and Eloise could not distinguish one from another, so we could use several different towels daily (for sanitary purposes).

When Eloise was suffering most, she would wrap the towel tightly around her and try to sleep. When she woke up, she would drape it over her head. She looked like a nun (an ugly one, no doubt). There were times when she sucked on a corner of the towel, and when she wasn't doing anything special with it, she just held it next to her body. She was never out of contact with her towel. Even during our daily exchanges she would not let go of one towel until she had a firm grasp on another.

Eloise used towels as a substitute person, just as Linus does in the wonderful comic strip "Peanuts." In the wild, Eloise would rarely have been out of contact from her mother, but in captivity she was raised as a human baby. She was picked up and put down several times a day, and that treatment had taken its toll. She needed her security towel as much as Linus needed his blanket. To say she was attached to her towel would be an understatement. She fell apart if she couldn't have it. This kind of behavior is an example of a love or liking of the subanimal, and it demonstrates that animals can attribute value to an inanimate object.

I am happy to say that the day came when Eloise's virus abated and she was able to return to her own cage in the collection where she could play with and touch other members of her own species. The day also came when Eloise no longer reached for a towel-companion. She found that she had animal-friends to take its place.

Affection

I took care of Sally the Orangutan, and she was an affectionate ape (at least for some people). I had a great relationship with her. She loved to have her back rubbed and her arms scratched. She would reward you with a gentle kiss on your hand for the kindness should you choose to take a little time with her.

Sally had one hang-up: she hated men with beards or mustaches. Although she was normally gentle and kind, she would go bonkers if anyone with a beard or mustache came near her. Some people theorized that she had been cruelly treated by a person with facial hair. I didn't agree with that because I felt that if it were true, she would cower or show signs of fear. But she didn't show fear; she was just out-and-out aggressive. Given the chance, Sally would attack anyone with a hairy face. The truth is, like many humans I know, she was prejudiced. We never could figure out why she loved some and hated others, but she did, and it was plain to see.

Not only did Sally show affection for some humans, she was also affectionate to her own species. Orangutans are not the least loyal to just one animal when they mate. They are promiscuous, but they do have favorites. Sally's "main man" was Eli, and he was the John Wayne of the orangutans in the zoo. Their relationship was planned from the beginning; neither had a choice of mate. They were just locked up together in the same cage.

Eli was 14 years old when he began to show any interest in Sally; she was in her early thirties. (I always kidded her about being a cradle robber.) During breeding season I saw Sally become affectionate. She and Eli acted just like a courting couple would. She touched Eli's hand gently, patted him, hugged him, and kissed him. When she finally learned how to take care of her babies and they could be left with her for her to raise, she was affectionate with them too.

One of my favorite memories is that of Sally in a rubber tub with one of her many newborns. She tenderly took it by its two tiny hands, lifted it into the air, and looked at it with love and pride. Then she lowered it and held it delicately to her breast and patted it. I dearly wish I could have captured that moment on film.

When animals love their young, that is affection. When they touch for comfort or to demonstrate warm feelings, that is affection too.

Friendship

Friendship is a wonderful kind of love. It is distinguished by the possession of common interests, but it is the kind of love that you see least in animals because it has no survival value. There is so much competition among animals for food that they are not as likely to have friends in the wild.

You are more likely to see friendships form between younger animals that do not have to compete for food. I have seen orangutans and chimpanzees, animals that had been raised in the zoo, form grand friendships. I have seen a litter of tigers wrestle and play all day and then sleep on top of each other until they were rested enough to play again.

In a zoo where there is more than enough food for all, you will see animals that enjoy each other's company pair off and spend a good deal of time together. I have seen gorillas eating their favorite food and then offer some to a cage mate. Jane Goodall the famous animal behaviorist that worked for the National Geographic Society noticed the pure and simple friendship between two male chimps that ran around together constantly. They would defend each other in any skirmishes that arose.

Jesus said that the greatest love a person can show is to die for his friends (*see* John 15:13). Dian Fossey's gorillas would defend their group to the death if they had to. One day, her beloved Digit, a noble male mountain gorilla, did just that, and the world mourned his death. If you have not read the book or seen the movie *Gorillas in the Mist*, you really must do so—but be prepared to be angry and brokenhearted when you do.

Friendship is the least-observed human love. Most of us have many acquaintances, but we have few friends. Our fallen nature mediates against it. We find it hard to trust, forgive, risk, ask, or give. Many people claim not to have the time it takes to be friends with another person. We compete in the marketplace and the workplace, and that makes friendships difficult. Jealousy and envy trouble our relationships and make true friendships difficult to form and keep.

I believe animals have friendships, but, as with humans, an animal is more likely to have acquaintances than true friends. An animal's problem is one of survival, whereas the problem with humans is their fallen nature.

Romance

Romance can be seen everywhere in the animal kingdom. Most animals have courtship rituals, and we can observe the romantic interludes that occur before mating.

These are wonderful. For example, the bower bird from Australia is your basic swinging single. He builds a little single's pad on the ground with sticks and straw and then paints it with blueberry juice so that it appeals to the chick he brings home with him. If she likes it, they go to nest. It's no long-term thing, you understand, just a short-term affair with no strings and no commitment. It's just one of those it-was-nice-while-it-lasted things.

Rattlesnakes perform an elaborate ballet before mating. It is a ritual of courtship. They mate and crawl away. It's just a one-shot deal, over before it begins.

The female black widow spider is four times as large as the male, who is not black at all, but white and gold. She is a deadly huntress and knows every inch of her web by feel. She is blind. When the male comes to court her, he plucks the web at a constant rhythm. It is his song of love, and it calms the throbbing black temptress. She quietly awaits his approach. Every few steps he plucks his song again to ensure that he is not mistaken for just any old housefly or moth. When he arrives beside her, he strokes her with his delicate front leg and begins the mating process. He is exhausted after mating. In his weakened condition he usually stumbles as he attempts to exit the web. The irregular vibrations trigger the black widow's instincts to kill, and he is quickly overtaken. Without emotion she adds him to her macabre pantry of stored delicacies. Well, males are a dime a dozen, anyway.

There are, however, some real, lasting romances in the wild kingdom. God has created a host of animals that mate for life: wolves, coyotes, foxes, parrots, penguins, geese, and swans are a sampling.

When I was at the zoo, the phone in the health center rang one day and the senior keeper of the bird section asked if we could take a look at a female coscoroba swan. These are rare swans, smaller and more delicate than their larger cousins. He told us that the other workers in that section had noticed that her ability to walk was deteriorating. Now she could only stumble a few steps before toppling forward into the mud at the edge of the zoo lake.

When we arrived at the lake we saw those very symptoms. Our veterinarian, Dr. Bernstein, who was an excellent vet, said, "I'm not prepared to make a diagnosis until we've done some testing." The bird keepers caught her and put her in a gunnysack. Her head and neck slid through a hole in the bottom, but her body was snug and comfortable inside the bag for the ride to the health center. She could not thrash around and injure herself while in the sack.

The male coscoroba swan to whom she was pairbonded was beside himself and didn't know how to defend her. He stayed in the water offshore and honked and whistled as we drove away. I noticed that the female had her eyes fixed on him all the way to the truck, and she answered his cries with some of her own. It was a sad parting. "We'll try to get you home as soon as possible, sweetheart," I said as she cried on the way to the health center.

We tried every test known to man but could not form an honest theory explaining why the swan could not walk. We did blood work, looked for bruises, and X-rayed her, but the tests only served to frustrate us because they didn't provide any clues. The swan frustrated us even more by refusing her food. I put her in a tub of hot water daily to help the circulation in her legs and rubbed them down for the same reason.

Day after day we watched her decline. There didn't seem to be any particular reason for it. She looked so sad. Most of the time she just lay quietly with her head turned to the wall and her neck curved so that she looked terribly depressed. One day Dr. Bernstein said, "Boys, she looks lonely. Swans mate for life, don't they?"

"Yes," I answered, anticipating what he was going to say.

Sure enough, Dr. Bernstein said, "Call the bird section and ask them if they could catch the male coscoroba for us. I think she could use a little company. I bet that's why she went off her feed."

I called the bird section just as they were getting ready to call me. They said that the male was on a hunger strike too, most likely protesting the removal of his mate. They asked if they could bring him up to the center.

The reunion was classic. As soon as they saw each other they began honking and whistling and started a head-and-neck bobbing ritual that I assume was a way of reestablishing their bond. In no time they were lying next to each other, eating like they had never eaten before. The female immediately began to improve. Two weeks later she was normal.

I still wonder what caused her problem, but her recovery is proof positive that the body is a remarkable thing. Whatever it was that had paralyzed her had passed. And it was a joy to watch the two swans; they were classic lovers. From the first day they came together at the health center I named them Cary and Deborah after Cary Grant and Deborah Kerr, stars in my all-time favorite love story *A Love Affair to Remember*. In the story, Deborah Kerr becomes paralyzed and is separated from Cary Grant for a while. They are both miserable but finally get back together and live happily ever after. That's exactly what happened to the swans, who were no less in love and completely bonded "till death did them part."

Animals love just as humans love. They die for each other. They help each other. They mourn for each other, give and receive affection, form friendships, like inanimate objects and attach value to them. They love in the same ways we love. God loves them too. His *agape* love makes the animals what they are and can transform us into what we should be. Animals have no need to improve; they don't sin. But God provides for them just as He does for us, except that His care for us is a different care: it is specially designed according to our needs.

C. S. Lewis reveals a great truth in his book *The Four Loves*. He lets us know that our loves are subject to our fallen nature; they are unpredictable and unchangeable. We tire of things. Our affections change. We lose friends. Our romances crumble.

He also points out that when we know Christ and we own His love, His love is in a position to rule our loves. His love can put things in balance and protect our loves. With His help, we can love people. We can learn to put others first (a behavior that seems strange to our age). Our friendships become better and our romances become more complete when we subject our wonderful but frail loves to God's unchanging and mighty love.

The apostle John wrote, "How great is the love the Father has lavished on us, that we should be called children of God! And that is what we are! The reason the world does not know us is that it did not know him. Dear friends, now we are children of God, and what we will be has not yet been made known. But we know that when he appears, we shall be like him, for we shall see him as he is" (1 John 3:1-2 NIV). The apostle also said, "This is [God's] command: to believe in the name of his Son, Jesus Christ, and to love one another as he commanded us. Those who obey his commands live in him, and he in them. And this is how we know that he lives in us: We know it by the Spirit he gave us" (1 John 3:23-24).

The bottom line is that God is love. You may have a measure of human love, but until you know the love of God through Jesus, what you know is a faint reflection of what's available. If you know the Lord, then you know that what I am saying is true. If you don't, then trust Him today . . . and be loved as you have never been loved before.

Chapter Twenty

The Theme Building

The Los Angeles Zoo was opened in September of 1966. It began its marbled history as the world's fifth-largest zoo and is the only zoo in modern history that was actually opened as a major zoo. In addition, it had several distinctions. One was that we accumulated more rare and endangered animals than any other zoo in the world. Another was that by the end of our third year, 52 percent of our collection was breeding annually. Those two statistics were very prized in the zoo world and commanded an early respect. But they also engendered a fair amount of jealousy.

There were many criticisms leveled against the Los Angeles Zoo when it was first built. Some were justified and some were not. For starters, it was built on a golf course which had produced a fair amount of revenue for the city, whereas the zoo lost a bundle every year. Also, the newly planted grounds made it look like a desert. During the first few summers the sun fried anybody who was foolish enough to come without some sort of shade, and visitors were blinded by the stark grey exhibits wherever they went. The zoo was often accused of being a concrete jungle. And it was.

The zoo was often criticized for its lack of showmanship as well. The supervisors resented presenting animals in acts of any kind. Their philosophy was that a zoo was an educational institution and ought not to pander to man's baser desires to be entertained when he ought to be educated.

The zoo was divided into nine sections: North America, South America, Africa, Australia, and Eurasia comprised the first five. Then there were the specialty sections: aquatics, birds, reptiles, and the children's petting zoo and nursery. The public rejected this arrangement at first because it made seeing their favorite type of animal more difficult. If you liked monkeys, for instance, you would have to visit Africa, Eurasia, and South America to see them all, and in so doing you would have also seen a number of animals you didn't want to see.

In the middle of the zoo stands its most prominent architectural feature—the Theme Building. It is on a rise that overlooks a fair portion of the main zoo, and its twin spires ascend ten stories into the sky. It is African, Indian, and Asian in appearance and really does set the architectural mood for the rest of the zoo. But what the Theme Building really turned out to be was an extremely expensive roof with a dirt floor. You see, the committee that worked with the architect could not agree on what should go under the magnificent roof. The architect was able to convince them that they could decide on that later. As for now, he said, it set the theme and was too important to his concept to be left out. And so it was built.

As time passed, the debate raged on. Some people thought the Theme Building should be turned into an expensive restaurant, others a gift shop, and some an educational center. Year followed year and all that the roof ever achieved was to provide shade for picnickers. Inexpensive benches were placed here and there under its ample eaves and zoo patrons simply sat there and ate lunches they had furnished for themselves.

In the zoo's first 20 years of existence, hundreds of additions and changes were made. Waterfalls and expensive rock works are everywhere. The trees are tall and full and provide more than enough shade for the zoo patrons at any hour of the day. The animal collection is rare and beautiful, and not many people are complaining anymore. It really is a beautiful zoo, one of the very best. But you know what? The finest architectural monument at the zoo is still a million-dollar roof with a dirt floor. It hasn't changed at all. It stands empty after all these years. No one could decide what should go inside it, so empty it stays.

• • •

When I think about the Theme Building, it makes me wonder how many people go for 20 or 30 years without bringing something meaningful into their lives. The prophet Elijah spoke about this to his own people, who could not decide who to bring into their lives. His speech may be found in 1 Kings 18:21:

> Elijah came near to all the people, and said, "How long will you go limping with two different opinions? If the Lord is God, follow him; but if Baal, then follow him." And the people did not answer him a word.

We were designed to be God's architectural wonder. We were made to be the temple of the Holy Spirit. Are you standing empty without His presence? Are you existing without anything inside? If you haven't before, let Him build your life into something meaningful.

For some people, this may mean trusting Christ with their whole life, asking His forgiveness for their sins, and committing themselves to His kingship.

For those of us who have known Christ, this may mean inviting Him back to take up the process that He began when we first met Him. Revelation 3:20 pictures a Jesus standing at the door of a believer's life asking to be let in so that he might resume fellowship with us. It is evident that His desire is to be very close to us.

Whatever your circumstance, you can know this with certainty: Christ is one architect who won't leave you empty.

CHAPTER TWENTY-ONE

Never Again

Since early childhood, I have suffered under the illusion that if I could obtain a certian possession or experience, I would be fulfilled, completed, happy. I am now 47. You would think I would have wisened and grown beyond these periodic wanderings into fantasyland. But I have not.

The smell of a new car, the shiny cover of a new book, the high-resolution picture screen on a television, the sleek lines of a new camera—all these call to me like sirens of old called to sailors to steer their sailing ships into certain oblivion. For me, fighting these urges might compare to a reformed smoker's desire to light one up or a recovered alcoholic's desire to feel the warmth of whiskey as it sears the throat and settles into the system.

My *needs* have always been met, but never my *wants*. My wants seem endless. You would know that if you had ever watched me come alive leafing through the Sears catalog—one of my favorite pastimes.

I have had some strange wants fulfilled and am grieved to report that I was never ever made happy by them. In fact, they are now an embarrassment to me. Let me tell you the worst experience I had with a want. It happened 28 years ago and still has a humbling effect whenever I recall it.

As a sophomore at Los Angeles Pacific College, I was living in a small one-bedroom apartment with two stable and godly young men who were both seniors at the same Christian college. I was engaged to Carol, my bride of 30+ years now. Those who knew me then thought of me as a responsible, thoughtful, and dedicated young man. However, those who knew me *well* knew I was capable of some unusual behavior.

It was during that period that I decided that the purchase of a bobcat would make me happy.

For weeks, I combed the classified section of the *Los Angeles Times* under the heading "Exotic Pets," hoping to see bobcat kittens for sale. One Friday afternoon I did find an ad, and my heart leaped for joy within me. My fingers trembled with anticipation as I dialed the phone number that was listed.

A woman answered and confirmed all my imaginings—that bobcats were indeed the new wave of the pet trade. She adored her female, and I could hardly take down directions to their home fast enough because she only had two kittens left.

I rushed down as fast as I could to find that the young kittens had been sold. But the couple again lifted my spirits by telling me they had a teenaged bobcat on their back porch, which they would be willing to part with at a bargain price. Under the spell of having an unusual pet, I did not notice that their house smelled like a giant, unchanged kitty-litter box.

As I held their pet, an affectionate adult female, I was certain beyond any doubt that a bobcat was what I wanted—or had to have! They took me to the back porch and there in a small carrying cage was a nearly grown female. When she saw me, she snarled and hissed. Her ears went down and she glared and growled the whole time we stood there talking.

The man assured me, "She'll tame down fine (*liar*). She just doesn't like being in a small cage like that." Did I mention that the man looked like he could be Anton LeVey's brother?

This wasn't what I had driven 40 miles to buy, but I was assured that she would tame down. Well, the bobcat looked healthy *(more like possessed)*. I paid $125 and left thinking what fun it would be to own a tame wildcat. I named her Tara. It seemed exotic and wild and fit perfectly.

When I finally got to our apartment, I was sad neither of my roommates were there to enjoy the surprise. I let the cat out of the carrying cage. She ran wildly around the room, searching for a place to escape. She opted to jump from the floor to the kitchen sink, then to a room divider just over the stove, about six feet above the ground. From there, she glared and continued to growl.

She would tame down, the man had said *(wrong!)*. I offered the bobcat assorted parts of an uncooked chicken, but she only batted them away with a haughty, who-needs-it attitude. Well, give her time. Bummer!

I had to leave the apartment to run an errand. While I was gone my roommate Fred came home, unaware that the apartment was occupied. He innocently walked to the kitchen sink to pour a glass of water. That's when he heard the low, rumbling growl behind him. He turned around slowly and found himself face to face with the she-devil bobcat I had purchased for just $125.

Fred backed slowly out of the kitchen, staying as close to the wall and as far away as he could from the evil presence that had claimed our apartment. Beads of perspiration formed all over his face as he let himself out the front door. Art would never get a bobcat, so Fred knew that I would be able to unravel the mystery. He waited for me to get home—safe on the porch.

I returned from my errand excited to see Fred sitting in front of our apartment. Something was obviously bothering him, so I asked him what was wrong. He looked at me as if I should know.

"Gary," he began in an exasperated way, "what's in our apartment? I went in to get something to drink and eat and began to hear a growl. I looked behind me, and ready to attack was some sort of wild animal. Is that a bobcat in there?"

"Yes, Fred, and she'll tame down soon. The family I bought her from said she's uptight from being in a small carrying cage. I got a great deal on her. She cost only $125."

"Gary, don't you think it would have been a good idea to ask Art and me before getting a bobcat? Personally, I liked our apartment better when I felt safe in it. I don't think she's going to tame down. Don't they call bobcats *wildcats?*"

"Come on, Fred. Tara will tame down, and you'll love her. You are so responsible and predictable, you need a little excitement in your life. You'll be able to tell your grandchildren you lived with a bobcat during your college days. Give it a try. Really, what can it hurt?"

We kept eye contact and Fred, a little stung wth the idea that he was too responsible and predictable, finally spoke. "Okay, we'll give it a try. If it doesn't work out, you and Tara will have to make other arrangements."

When we stepped into our small apartment, we were greeted by a significant odor. It was a good news, bad news thing. The good news was that Tara had used her kitty-litter tray. The bad news was that she needed a tray six times larger and deeper to achieve sanitation. Kitty litter and odor were everywhere. I'm not an optimist, but even I knew that this was not a good beginning: Fred didn't say anything but gave me a very skeptical look.

When Art got home he got a big laugh out of the whole deal and was more willing than Fred to give it a try. He laughed every time Tara growled at one of us, which she continued to do every day she lived with us, which was a little over a week.

Tara never allowed me to pet her or even touch her. Every effort ended with her taking a fearsome swipe at me, and then she would run and hide behind or under something. Most of the time though, she just stared down from her favorite haunt—the room divider above the kitchen. Fred and Art locked themselves in the bedroom at night and left me on the couch with Tara lurking somewhere in the darkness. Our apartment smelled like a giant kitty-litter box, and it was filled with tension.

Even an optimist usually knows when something isn't working. I knew the guys were anxious for me to admit that living in small quarters with a wild animal was not good. They wanted me to say, "Guys, you were right; this was a stupid thing to do." But I hate to admit it when I'm wrong, so it took a final straw.

Tara somehow got into the bathroom early in the morning when everybody else in the apartment needed to get ready for classes. She claimed it for her own and would not let any of us in for whatever reason. She was getting wilder and meaner each day. Even I was not sure whether or not she would attack. At any rate, all three of us left for class unwashed, unshaven, and undeodorized.

As he left, Fred spoke the words I knew were coming: "She has to go!"

When Art nodded, I shared something that was difficult and painful for me to say. "You guys are right. I never should have bought her."

I called the man who sold Tara to me; he was sad she wasn't working out. He said he knew a man who wanted her and would send him right over. *Man, everything was going to work out fine,* I thought. The man showed up and with a little effort—about an hour of terrifying running around—we finally got Tara back into her carrier. I told the man I'd sell her for only $125. He said that was more than a fair price, but he didn't have the money right then and would send it to me.

I didn't have much of a bargaining position, so I let him take the bobcat. A week passed, but no money came. I called the telephone number he had given me. Guess what? It was disconnected. I drove to the address he had given to me; he had been evicted.

My only satisfaction was that he had the bobcat.

And that's the only satisfaction that this story brings me because it highlights one of my greatest weaknesses, one I continue to fight: the subconscious conviction that a certain purchase will make me happy. I was 19 when all of this occurred. I am 30+ years older, and still at times I must fight to keep from being foolish and attempting to fill voids that are not there.

I am wiser now and know one thing for sure. If I live to be 100, I will never buy another bobcat.

Chapter Twenty-Two

Debt of Love

The stillness of the morning was violated by the shrill ring of the zoo's hospital phone. I picked it up. "Zoo Health Center, Richmond speaking."

"Richmond, Ray Landers on this end. My boss said to call you guys and see if Doc Bernstein could come down and take a look-see at the baby bison. His right front leg is all swelled up near the hoof, and he's limping bad. His leg don't look broke, more like it's infected."

"Ray, the doc's free and we can be down there in about 15 minutes. I think it's a given we'll have to grab the calf. He'd weigh in at about 200 or 225 pounds, don't you think? He's big enough to be a handful. Could you round up a couple of the guys from your section to help us?"

"I don't think grabbing the calf is going to be the worst of things," exclaimed Ray. "Separating him from his mama is gonna be the test, don't ya know? Might take a minute or two. I never saw a mom and baby so bonded."

"We'll help when we get there," I assured him. Then I conveyed we had whatever time it would take to help the calf.

When I told Doc Bernstein about the bison calf, he was excited that there was something to do. We quickly threw together what we thought we might need and headed for the North America section.

While we were riding in the truck, Doc shared some great stuff on bison. "The buffalo are great animals. They have always been one of my favorites. When the Pilgrims landed on Plymouth Rock, there were 75 million buffalo. They were the staple of the Native American economy. As soon as our government realized that fact, they called for the buffalo's eradication. People were told to shoot them from trains, the U.S. Cavalry was told to drive them off cliffs, anything to get rid of them so we could 'manage the Injuns, force them into reservations.' By 1895 there were only 400 bison left. If it hadn't been for some Colorado ranchers and a Blackfoot Indian named Samuel Walking Coyote, they would probably have been shot out of existence. We're back up to about 30,000 now, so they are making a nice comeback. Next to the bald eagle, I think they are the best symbol of America's wildlife."

Doc Bernstein was a great veterinarian and a great guy. The zoo staff referred to him as a keeper's vet. That was to say he was not only good for the animals but for the keeping staff, too. He always took the time to explain to the keepers what he was doing and why. The keeping staff returned the favor by respecting and honoring him. There was nothing we wouldn't do for him because we were sure there was nothing he wouldn't do for us, including sharing freely from his vast and ecclectic store of knowledge.

We arrived at the barn, and three enthusiastic animal keepers in the mood for a little adventure were there to meet us. "At your service, Doc," said Ray. "I got the female and calf in the barn. We'll separate them when you're ready."

Doc Bernstein thought a minute and said, "Maybe it would be best to isolate the calf and let the cow outside. What do you think?"

"Consider it done, Doc." Ray and the two keepers quickly disappeared into the barn, and in seconds we could hear the hooves of the cow and calf shuffling from stall to stall inside. As we gathered our medical equipment, we saw one of the sliding doors open, and the excited and agitated cow exited by herself. We now knew the calf was isolated, and we could do our thing.

Once inside the barn we made brief plans. This was not a risky moment, to be sure, but there was always the chance we might hurt an excited animal if we did not observe some basic common sense. We wanted everyone to be sure they understood their role. I was assigned to be the first in and to push the calf against the wall. Then, pretty much all at once, Ray and the two keepers would grab the head, the front legs, and the back legs. We would slowly lower the calf to the floor. I would then lay across the body to minimize thrashing, and the back legs would be extended so no one would be kicked. Ray would hold the calf's head in his lap to keep the animal from hurting itself. The remaining would immobilize the front legs and keep them extended for Doc to perform his exam and treatment, if necessary. That's just how it happened. It went down real smooth—for about a minute.

Outside the barn we could hear the mother pacing back and forth and mooing loudly to the calf. The calf answered back as if to say, "I'm in here, Mom. I'm in here!"

Doc Bernstein began to examine the right front hoof, quickly exclaiming, "There's the problem. It's a good-sized nail jammed in the hoof. Those construction guys dropped a lot of nails before they left."

Doc reached into his black bag and pulled out a medical instrument that look like pliers. Then he deftly pulled the nail out of the hoof, and the calf stiffened and screamed out in pain. Dr. Bernstein showed us the nail, about two inches long, and reached back into his bag for antibiotics, tetnus toxoid, peroxide, and betadine for flushing out the wound.

It was at that very moment that our plans unraveled.

Suddenly the barn door was blasted out of its lower track. It swung upward in an arc, knocking the doc and one of the keepers flat on the shavings-covered concrete floor of the barn. Light flooded in, and the head and shoulders of the calf's mother became all too visible. She was forcing her way in to save the life of her calf, or so we assumed. It was clear she'd be fully inside with us in seconds.

The keepers moved quickly to climb the slats of the stall walls, and the doc and I pushed them to safety. When they were clear, I turned to Doc and our eyes locked. He yelled. "Get out now!" I hesitated, thinking it was my job to protect him, and he yelled fiercely, "NOW!" I felt his strong arms pushing me to safety as I climbed up and out of the stall. When I looked back down, the doc was looking at the enraged cow. She was in the stall with her sights set on him.

He was out of time by a second. With quick thinking, he dove under the hay feeder that was bolted to the wall slats. Covering his head with his arms, he prepared to be bashed and gored. The female charged and tried to hook him with a horn, but her horn caught the hay feeder and swung her head away from Doc. Backing up, charging again, and thumping him with her nose, she continued to struggle to find a way to do some real damage to avenge the pain caused to her calf.

Ray opened all the stall and barn doors to give the mother and calf an easy way out of the barn. It was good thinking, but the mother was not distracted.

None of us were about to stand by and watch Doc Bernstein get killed. He had been willing to lay his life on the line for us, and it was time for us to return the favor. We grabbed shovels and rakes and rushed back into the stall where we pounded on her furiously, finally getting her attention. She looked dazed, then looked about for her calf, which had run outside. Not seeing the calf, she ran outside to look for it. We were very grateful, because the sum total of us was not her equal battle. Should we have joined in battle, we would have been toast.

• • •

When we had run back into the stall, it was to pay back a debt of love. It had not been as a result of a logical decision. If we were logical, we would have simply thought, *Tough break, Doc. Luck of the draw. Bummer.* But ours was a very emotional response, and the emotion was love. Or maybe way down deep, it was a logical response. We do reap what we sow in the good sense of the saying also.

Whatever the case, we had just had a crash course in true sacrifice from Dr. Bernstein. It had paid off big time. Other than a pair of broken glasses, he stood up without a scratch.

This had truly been a bonding experience, and I shall not forget it, ever. I shall also not forget the sacrifice enacted on my behalf 2,000 years ago.

Jesus said, "Greater love has no man than this, that a man lay down his life for his friends" (John 15:13). Indeed, Jesus would know.

In the classic words from *Sister Act II.* "What have you done for Him lately?"

CHAPTER TWENTY-THREE

What's It to You?

There was no doubt in my mind that my wife, Carol, was interested when I confessed that I was finding myself attracted to a 24-year-old redhead named Sally. I shared that Sally was short, had beautiful brown eyes, was extremely affectionate, and was absolutely brilliant. I told her how Sally's auburn-red hair trailed gently down her back, arms, legs, and feet, and she even had some on her head. Carol was entertained when I admitted that Sally was an orangutan. Sally was under my care at the zoo's health center while her assigned mate, Eli, was being treated for tuberculosis in an adjacent cage.

Sally and Eli were as different as night and day. Sally was a butterball, sweet, helpful, gentle, and smart as a whip. Eli was grouchy, calculating, meaner than sin, and stronger than an ox.

Let me tell you some stories that will help you to know them better. Sally was my favorite animal, and still is, so I will begin with her.

Any keepers worth their salt will offer their great apes something to do. In the wild, these animals spend their time looking for food and shelter. Since those things are provided in a zoo, there is nothing for these intelligent and sensitive apes to do but watch an endless stream of people watching them. If you could imagine watching a movie that had no change of scenery, an everchanging cast, and no plot, then you have conceived what a great ape's existence might be like without a creative keeper. Lack of occupation leads to abnormal and aggressive behavior.

I loved to give Sally things to do because she always participated so enthusiastically. Problem-solving was her forte. So I gave her lots to solve.

I would line up 20 peanuts exactly three feet out from the bars of her cage and give her a bath towel. Then Sally would fish for the peanuts by repeatedly casting the towel over them. Little by little she would drag them one at a time to the cage and place them in a neat little pile. She was so decent and orderly that I'm sure she was a Presbyterian.

I'll never forget the day of Sally's great discovery. I set up the peanuts in the normal fashion and handed her a white bath towel. She carefully unfolded it and draped it over her considerable lap, studying it thoughtfully. Then she gave me that "Eureka!" look. She got up quickly and scooted to her drinker, dragging the towel behind her. She looked back at me, and her expression told me she was onto something big. She dipped the towel in and out of the drinker several times until she was satisfied that it was thoroughly soaked. Then she wrung out the excess water. She ambled over to where I had placed the 20 peanuts and cast her wet towel over five of them. She retrieved them with just one effort. I was astounded. To tell you the truth, I'm not sure that I would have reasoned that a wet towel would have increased my advantage. But Sally did. Sally viewed food as her great necessity. And you know what they say: "Necessity is the mother of invention."

Sally's love for food bordered on lust, and she developed whole routines to gain our empathy and attention. She would begin with lip smacking and graduate to body slapping. When we looked at her she would smile a gargantuan smile and point to her mouth. If nothing else worked she would croak forth with grunts and barking sounds that clearly displayed her frustration. One day she took a more direct approach.

I was passing by Sally's cage to deliver a bunch of grapes to some primates at the back of the health center. Suddenly, her mighty hand shot through the bars and grasped my arm with an iron grip. She gently but firmly pulled me close to the bars and pointed to the grapes. She smiled. There was no doubt in my mind that she wanted the grapes, and I found that a perfectly convenient time to let her have them. She took them in a most ladylike manner and delicately laid them on her sleeping bench. Keeping my arm firmly in her grasp, she reached out for the hand which had held the grapes, drew it slowly to her mouth, and kissed it. Then she patted me on the back as if to say, "Keep up the good work."

Sally was also helpful. She delighted in scraping up her leftover food into a neat pile and dropping it just outside her cage. On one morning I filled a bucket with warm soapy water and set it right next to her cage. I showed her how to clean the bars of her cage using a bath towel and then gave her the towel. She worked diligently for 40 minutes scrubbing, rinsing, and wringing. She cleaned all the bars, her sleeping bench, and her holding cage. That little effort won her a vanilla malt.

When Sally was finally allowed to be caged with Eli she became a prolific breeder. She is the mother of at least seven offspring. But her first birth was the most dramatic. Her baby Jonathan was born still encased in the placental sack. She had no idea that she needed to remove it, and we all watched in terror as she sat doing nothing while her newborn was dying from lack of oxygen. Finally, Dr. Sedgwick rushed in, at some personal risk, and took the baby. Nearly five minutes had passed before he tore the tiny orangutan from its birthing sack. The baby was cool, still, and hadn't taken a breath. Dr. Sedgwick began CPR and stimulated the body with deliberate massage. Still no breathing or heartbeat. Dale Thompson, the keeper who was assisting Dr. Sedgwick, asked, "What do we do now?"

The heroic vet looked up long enough to say, "We don't give up. We never give up."

He injected a heart stimulant and the baby stiffened in response. All who were present cheered and then held their breath to see what would come of the doctor's last chance to retrieve the baby's ebbing life. The heartbeat was weak at first, and then it began to increase in volume and regularity. Jonathan would live. He would always be a little slow because of the severe oxygen deficit he suffered at birth, but he was alive and well and today is bringing a great deal of pleasure to thousands of zoo visitors.

Sally is really something. Visitors to the Los Angeles Zoo still watch her perform her hilarious food routines. She has added a new gesture that I had never noticed while she was under my care. She uses her hand to shade her eyes from the glare of the sun.

Eli was nothing like Sally. He spent every waking moment looking for opportunities to pull keepers through the bars of his cage. We had to be watchful while walking near his cage because he had the kind of strength necessary to tear a man's arm off. A San Francisco zookeeper lost his arm to a large male orangutan during a careless moment.

I once saw Eli perform a feat of strength that made me a believer. Eli's cage was positioned next to a garage door that was opened every morning to ventilate the health center. When the door was opened the spring was extended precariously close to Eli's cage. Eli was just able to twang the spring with his longest massive finger. No matter where I worked in the health center I could hear the monotonous twang as he plucked at it with regularity.

In the back of my mind, I knew that someday he would grasp the spring with his whole hand. I did not think that I would actually see it happen, but I did. Eli was in late adolescence and was growing rapidly toward adulthood.

I was heading back to the orangutans' area after checking on the other animals under my care at the center. When I rounded the corner, I stopped in amazement. Eli had fully grasped the spring and was pulling it into his cage. He resembled a giant, hairy Robin Hood pulling a long bow to its limit. The whole garage door assembly bent towards the cage, and then he grabbed that. He pulled with all his might and ended up pulling bolts through a cracking and splintering four-by-four. By the time we were able to remove the assembly, he had tied the metal spring into several knots.

After I witnessed that incident, I added a foot or two onto the already respectful distance that I walked from Eli's cage. And there were more incidents to follow.

Eli delighted in breaking things. One day he managed to stuff his whole body underneath his sleeping bench, which was welded securely to the bars of his cage about 18 inches off the floor. Eli then flexed every muscle in his powerful body. The two-inch by six-inch boards that were bolted to the sleeping bench cracked, then shattered all over the floor of his cage. Eli chose the largest board and fashioned it into a lever. He jammed the lever between the chain that secured the door and the bars of his cage. He pulled with all of his strength but succeeded only in breaking the lever. We were glad.

The most frightening incident occurred one day at feeding time at the health center. It was one o'clock in the afternoon and the vet and I were just finishing our lunch. A bloodcurdling, bone-chilling scream exploded the afternoon stillness and we looked at each other, both knowing what was happening. Ken, the keeper in the cage room, was in Eli's grasp. If we didn't get there quick, Ken's chances of survival were slim to none.

We leaped out of our chairs and headed for the cage room with reckless abandon. I veered off to grab the capture gun that always intimidated Eli. He wouldn't know if it was loaded or not. The doctor unlocked the cage room door and we burst through the opening together. Ken was screaming at the top of his lungs and we were hoping that we were not too late to save a hand or fingers. As we rounded the corner we saw that other help had arrived before us. Ken's senior keeper was poised to swing a shovel at Eli's hand. Ken had managed to turn his arm so that Eli could not pull it through the bars. Eli was trying his best to turn Ken's arm while the senior keeper was trying to get a line on hitting Eli's hand with the shovel. The senior took a powerful swing. This was no time to hold back. Eli was mean but he wasn't stupid, and he removed his hand at the last possible second. The shovel connected with Ken's arm, causing him much more injury than Eli had.

Ken rolled backwards a safe distance from the cage, looked up at the senior keeper, smiled a relieved smile, and said, "Whose side are you on anyway?"

Eli wouldn't let you like him. Because of his meanness I gave him satisfactory, but not exceptional, care. There were many times that Sally procured treats that I denied Eli. I didn't mind cleaning up after Sally when I had given her a magazine to look at, but I did Eli. The bottom line was that Sally was easy to love but Eli wasn't. I really had to force myself to be nice to him.

As time passed, however, I came to learn the difference between the good keepers and the great. The great simply gave their best to all their animals no matter how the animals performed.

• • •

I'm sure that God expects the same from Christians. Jesus shares some words that haunt me when I try to apply them to my life. These words are found in Luke 6:27-36. See how they affect you.

> I say to you that hear, love your enemies, do good to those who hate you, bless those who curse you, pray for those who abuse you. To him who strikes you on the cheek, offer the other also; and to him who takes away your coat do not withhold even your shirt. Give to every one who begs from you; and of him who takes away your goods do not ask them again. And as you wish that men would do to you, do so to them.
>
> If you love those who love you, what credit is that to you? For even sinners love those that love them. And if you do good to those who do good to you, what credit is that to you? For even sinners do the same. And if you lend to those from whom you hope to receive, what credit is that to you? Even sinners lend to sinners, to receive as much again. But love your enemies, and do good, and lend, expecting nothing in return; and your reward will be great, and you will be sons of the Most High; for he is kind to the ungrateful and the selfish. Be merciful, even as your Father is merciful.

I don't know about you, but I find it frightfully easy to be nice to people who are nice to me. I find myself cheerfully answering the phone to look good for someone who's calling and yet be distant, trite, and brief to my wife, children, and other people that I so often take for granted.

The truth is, I constantly have to take inventory as to who I am being nice to. To be like Christ means, at minimum, to offer *everyone* kindness and to wish them well.

Will you take inventory with me . . . today?

Chapter Twenty-Four

A Boa Constrictor's Loose

It was the middle of September, and it was hot. For two consecutive weeks the temperatures had been resting in the high nineties every afternoon. I was booked to speak in Barstow at a Campus Life Saturday night rally, and I had to be there at 6:00 P.M. Barstow is in the Mojave Desert, and they had been seeing temperatures soar to 110 degrees Fahrenheit.

My car didn't have air conditioning, and I was supposed to take a large South American redtail boa constrictor named Samson with me. Hundreds of young people would be disappointed if he did not show, but I was concerned because the car might reach temperatures beyond Samson's level of tolerance. I shared my dilemma with my wife, Carol, and she reminded me that her mother had offered the use of their air-conditioned Dodge Dart if we needed it.

I picked up the car, loaded slide projectors and slides into the trunk, and put Samson on the front seat next to me. I carried Samson in a pillowcase that always attracted attention. It had "Juvenile Hall" written across the top of it because that's where it had come from. Carol had gotten it from her sister Darla, who had helped at Juvenile Hall while she was in nursing school. The pillowcase was well worn by a lot of ill-behaved teenaged heads. I was aware that it would soon be time to get a new one, but not aware enough, as it turned out.

I allowed two and one-half hours to get to Barstow. Because of the efficiency of the air conditioner, Samson and I arrived rested and ready to go. As soon as I opened the car door to get out, the heat hit us like a blast furnace. I was sure that Samson would never have made the trip alive without the air conditioning.

I was greeted by wonderfully friendly people who were glad to help me unload everything but Samson. They decided I could accomplish that without their help. But I was used to that response. People would feel differently after the program when they saw young children petting and holding the docile predator without incident.

The program opened with music, singing, and announcements. In no time they were introducing me. "Ladies and gentlemen, all the way from the Los Angeles Zoo with a fascinating program illustrated with beautiful slides is our guest speaker, Gary Richmond. Let's give him a warm Barstow welcome."

I hoped it wouldn't be too warm, because the air conditioner in the building was inadequate for the heat wave outside. Though the crowd seemed acclimated to the 87-degree gymnasium, Samson and I were not. I was drenched in perspiration, and Samson was trying his best to get out of the pillowcase so he could find a cooler place to rest.

I was glad when the lights were turned out so that the enormous sweat rings that had appeared on my shirt would no longer be visible. My talk went fine, and they were an enchanting and responsive audience. When the lights were again turned on, I leaned to the microphone and said, "If you will relax for one minute, I will bring out a friend of mine that many of you have been waiting to meet." I stepped down off the stage to get Samson, but my heart sank as I felt the empty pillowcase. Samson was somewhere in a crowd of 300 people, and I didn't know where.

I stepped back to the microphone and said, "Ladies and gentlemen, I'm going to ask you to trust me completely for your good, my good, and Samson the boa constrictor's good. You need to know that he is very tame. He has never bitten anyone ever. You have nothing to fear when I say he has escaped."

There was a bit of murmuring.

"Do not leave your seats," I continued, "but please look under them. If you see him, raise your hand, and I will come and pick him up." It was funny to see everybody bend over slowly to see if Samson had chosen them. Nobody raised a hand, and some people began to think they were being put on.

"One second," I asked. I jumped off the stage and walked around the crowd to see if Samson was against the wall. As soon as I saw a stack of gymnastic mats, I knew where I would find him. I pulled the mats away from the wall, and there he was. As I picked up the snake, the crowd clapped and cheered. There was suddenly a circus atmosphere, and everyone enjoyed that all's-well-that-ends-well moment. Scores of people held and touched Samson. He turned out to be the highlight of the evening.

Later when I picked up the pillowcase, I found the large hole through which he had escaped. He must have flexed and torn the case in the heat of the evening. Before putting him back in the pillowcase, I tied a knot at the end that had the hole. We loaded the car, and I was off for home. It was 9:30, and I expected to get home about midnight.

I turned on the radio, and as I sat back to relax, I reached over and patted Samson. I patted him for two reasons. First, I appreciated the addition he had been to the program and told him so, although, being a snake, he had no ears and could not hear me. Second, I patted him to make sure that he was still in the pillowcase. If he had escaped once, he could do it again. I could feel his muscular body tense to my touch, then relax.

There is nothing more wonderful than a California desert night. The temperature was now in the low eighties, and I was intoxicated by the fragrance of the sand, sagebrush, and yuccas that were silhouetted against the black-velvet, star-studded sky. The windows were down, and there was virtually no traffic. Even at 70 miles per hour (the speed limit then), the ride seemed relaxed and the progress seemed minimal. But that was okay because I was enraptured by the number of stars spread out before me. They looked three-dimensional. In Los Angeles, the lights of the city all but block out the stars, so it was refreshing to enjoy God's spectacular handiwork at its best.

I then reached over to pat Samson again, and my heart skipped a beat. The pillowcase was empty.

I pulled over to the side of the road and skidded to a stop. I turned on the overhead light and began looking under the front seats and the dashboard without success. I begin to feel into places that I could not see, desperate to find the escape-artist snake. I noticed that the air-conditioner vents were large and suspected that Samson had crawled into one of them. I reached into them as far as I could. I did so with caution, because even though Samson was tame, sometimes tame snakes who have gotten free will make an exception to their normal behavior and bite to stay free.

I wondered where the air-conditioner vent led. I hoped that Samson hadn't crawled through and fallen onto the road. But he certainly did not seem to be in the car. I put my ear to the vents and held my breath to see if I could hear any movement. I could not. Samson was either gone or at rest.

Now this situation was not good for two reasons. One, Samson was not my snake, and two, this was not my car. I had always enjoyed a terrific relationship with my mother-in-law, but I felt that returning the car to her, not knowing for sure whether a large boa constrictor was a silent passenger who might turn up again in freeway traffic, could put a bit of a strain on that relationship. Who was I kidding? She'd never speak to me again. I was sick.

I started the car and headed for home. How was I going to tell my best friend, Dale, that I had lost his snake—that Samson may have been the victim of the next 18-wheeler to come down the highway? Samson a frisbee. What a horrible thought!

But was it more horrible than the thought of Samson still in the car, carefully hidden in 100-degree weather? The car could only be driven at night until we knew for sure where he was. If a snake Samson's size were to die undiscovered, he would begin to smell in a day and no one would be able to drive the car again. Nothing dies as convincingly as a snake. No odor approximates a dead snake. Look in the dictionary under *stench,* and you'll see a picture of a dead snake.

How was I going to tell Carol that Samson was lost in her mother's new car? I prayed for wisdom, the rapture, a silver tongue. Help!

When I got home, it was a little before midnight. Carol was still up, and she was very understanding. We got a flashlight and looked again to find Samson. When we didn't find him, I suggested that I ought to find an all-night garage so that I might at least ask a mechanic whether a snake could crawl through the vents and fall on the road. If not, then we could presume that Samson was still in the car, and we would have to keep it parked in shady places so that the heat wouldn't kill him.

I pulled into a gas station in Highland Park, a suburb of Los Angeles, and got out of the car. The all-night mechanic on duty greeted me and asked how he could help me. I wasn't sure how to begin. No matter how I framed my question, I was going to come off as some kind of nutball.

"I have a hypothetical question," I said hesitantly.

"Hypothetical?" he queried. I wondered if maybe he didn't know what hypothetical meant because most of his customers just had questions that were straightforward, normal, everyday questions. Shoot, I wished I had one.

I opened the passenger door and pointed to the air-conditioner vent, which was well illuminated, and asked, "If something about ten inches around, say as big as a large navel orange, crawled in this hole, would it be able to crawl all the way out of the car and drop onto the highway?" As I was speaking I knew I sounded a little irrational. I could see it in the mechanic's eyes. They had narrowed, and he had stepped back from the car.

"Jus' what's da sumpin' that's crawled in da vent?" he asked with a good deal of skepticism.

I didn't want to admit that a boa constrictor was loose in the car, so I said, "Something about the size of a big rat." Then I realized that anyone who didn't like snakes wouldn't likely be fond of big rats either. The whites of his eyes showed me that.

"They's a ten-inch-around rat in yo air vent?"

"Well, no," I admitted. "Something the size of a rat, a real big rat, is in there unless he was able to crawl through. If he could crawl through, then he's history. He's part of the pavement in the Mojave Desert."

The mechanic took another step back. "Les 'stablish sumpin'. Dis conversation is comin' to a quick halt les you tells me what in there. Sumpin' like a big rat don't sound like to me is a rat. What is in there?"

I was caught. "Well, I know this sounds kind of silly, but I work at the Los Angeles Zoo and I speak a lot to schools and organizations and church groups, and things like that. And I sometimes take my best friend's boa constrictor. . . ." That's when I lost him. He jumped away from the car.

"You means to tell me you almos' had me pokin' aroun' fo a big snake? You got dus' fo brains or sumpin'? I'm tellin' ya. Shoot, man, I can't believe it. Ya see's down the boulevard, 'bout fo blocks? Dey got an all-night guy, too. But ta tell ya de truth I think you on yo own. Close dat do of yo car. All right?"

I tried to put myself in his place, and I really could understand why he might be reluctant. Boy, was I feeling stupid. I pulled out of the driveway and began to go to the other gas station, but on the way my pride got the best of me. I knew I was going to look like a kook, and I couldn't face someone's incredulous expression one more time that night. I headed home.

I couldn't sleep much thinking what I was going to tell my mother-in-law. I thought for two hours, but nothing good came of it. I kept picturing her face with a lot of the whites of her eyes showing when I said, "Oh, Mom, did I mention Samson's loose in your car and we can't find him?"

We left the Dodge in the garage the next morning and drove to church in our own car. It was 80 degrees before 9:30 in the morning. Several of our friends got a kick out of our little dilemma. Carol and I asked the more mechanically inclined whether they thought Samson was in or out of the car, but there was no consensus. I left church in the unbearable heat feeling deflated. I wondered if even our garage would be too hot for Samson if he was still in the car.

When we got home, Carol started calling Dodge dealerships hoping that someone would help us to at least eliminate the possibility of escape. They were not sure, and on Sunday there were no members of the service department available to consult.

I went back to look in the car again, and while poking around I discovered that with some effort I could push my hand between the back seat and the side panel. Maybe Samson had crawled under the back seat.

I could not find the right combination of pushes and pulls to remove the seat, but Carol called a man at a dealership who gave her just the right combination. After he did, he said, "Ma'am, if I were you I wouldn't go anywhere near that car." But she did. With a push back, a pull up, and a pull forward, the back seat was free.

I carefully removed it and turned it upside down. Woven throughout the springs was the glossy, colorful, formidable serpent whose escape had provided the most humbling, harrowing, and exasperating 13 hours of my life. But it was over. Well, almost. I couldn't get him out of the springs.

We took the seat into our living room and left it upside down until Samson extricated himself. I picked him up, looked him in the eye, and said, "Gotcha, ya little devil." But he didn't hear me because snakes don't have ears. Snakes don't smile either, but I believe he looked a little proud of himself.

• • •

The apostle Paul promises that there is coming a day when the Lord "will bring to light the things now hidden in darkness" (1 Corinthians 4:5).

Many of us carry in our lives things that are like a loose boa constrictor. If they are not brought into the light and into subjection, they will lurk in the shadows of our lives until they hurt someone.

We are the most likely victims of the dragons within us. But our pride frequently prevents our doing what is right. We think that if we just let our dragons be, they will go away. But the trouble with dragons is that they love a willing habitat. Left undisturbed, they will grow and claim more and more territory.

How about you? How about me? Do we need to bring something into the light? Deal with it? Admit that it's there and slowing us down?

Is it a habit? Is it an old, undealt-with sin? Has it grown heavy with time? Have we wanted to share it with a pastor or a friend so that the curse of its persistent pain and pressure would leave us alone and we could be at peace again? Do that while the Spirit is prompting you. Do it before your resolve weakens and you find yourself pretending it will go away, even though it never has before.

If we don't bring it into the light, God will, and for our own good. He has proven to be good at serpent control, and we need to trust Him to help us after we are obedient.

CHAPTER TWENTY-FIVE

The Zoo's Worst Night

When I was 13 I walked across a graveyard at midnight with two of my closest friends. I think it was a rite of manhood, but I was never sure. Doug and Ronny pretended to be brave as did I, but when we told the story later to friends, we all confessed that we had been afraid. Not terrified, but afraid. I remembered that my heart began to pound when I realized that we were smack dab in the middle of about 10,000 dead bodies. I wondered if one of them might reach out of the ground and pull me into a casket for a little conversation.

As exciting as a graveyard is at midnight, it is no match for a large zoo at the same hour. Graveyards are full of imagination, zoos are reality. When you hear something growling in the night at a zoo, it comes from something real that you hope is still in its cage. Zoo roads twist and turn, winding on and on. Trees and bushes abound to conceal any hidden thing. The Los Angeles Zoo had so many animals escape in its early days that you never felt truly safe at night. I have been through the zoo on many nights for various reasons, and I would choose a graveyard over a nighttime zoo for recreation any time.

I often wondered how the night security guards kept their sanity while checking the zoo late at night month after month. I am sure one guard didn't fare so well. It was the zoo's worst night when he lost it, and he lost it big.

Hans Gruber said he didn't mind when he pulled night duty. He was, for the most part, a loner, not by his own choosing, I think, but because there was so much about him to avoid. Hans loved and collected guns. He was forever trying to get someone to listen to him expound on what a big hole a .44 caliber pistol could make in a person or animal. Hans also hated everyone, but he said it wasn't prejudice to say the things he did because what he said was fact. Once, while trying to demonstrate his openness and liberality, he said he would date Jewish women except he didn't want to take a chance on falling in love with one. Exasperated, I asked him why not. He floored me when he said that Jewish women age twice as fast as blond-haired German men and he didn't want anybody thinking he had married an old lady when he grew older. I asked him how he knew this to be true. He said it was just his observation after years of watching Jewish people and "regular people."

Still, I tried to be friendly with Hans because I felt sorry for him. I felt that was what God wanted me to do. Although there were some pretty good reasons for Hans to feel lonely, I still felt compelled to talk to him when he delivered the mail to the health center.

I frightened Hans one day when he was running down the Jewish people. He had just made a comment about big-nosed Jews when it dawned on him that my nose was large. He said, "By the way, Richmond, you're not Jewish, are you?" I just nodded yes and walked away as if I were disgusted. Because Jesus was in me, I felt that qualified me in some mysterious way to be a little Jewish. Hans was flustered, but he apologized. I told him that was okay. I said

I understood that he was raised to think the way he did about Jews, and I was used to people making fun of my nose. It was enlightening to see the way that he reacted to me after that. He wanted to be friends as we had been but wasn't quite sure that he could. I continued to be friendly but could feel the struggle within him when he was in my presence.

I finally decided to tell him that I was not Jewish but that I would be proud to be if I was. I told him that my Lord was Jewish and that the Jews were God's chosen people. I also asked Hans not to make negative comments about the Jewish people when he was around me because it hurt my feelings. He didn't after that, and we got along fine.

When Hans drew night duty, I rarely saw him. During those times I sort of missed our inane conversations and kidding.

No one knew that night duty was taking its toll on Hans, and he wouldn't admit it to anyone. Because he was frightened for his own safety, he had gone against zoo policy and begun carrying a gun in his security vehicle. He had been startled by transients and teenagers who had crawled over and under the fences into the zoo. Running into a ragged street person looking for food or a group of older teens crashing the zoo on a lark at 2:00 A.M. could take the wind out of anyone's sails.

In June of 1968 a blanket of fog settled over the Los Angeles Zoo every night. By 9:00 P.M., the visibility was about 40 feet, even with foglights. One evening Hans was on his second run, checking seven miles of interior zoo roads. He was more on edge than usual from the strain of driving under these conditions, and his eyes darted back and forth trying not to miss anything unusual. Even though it was cool outside, he was perspiring. When he finished his run, he reported in at the security office to visit the restroom and splash cool water in his face. He recorded in the log that everything was normal and told Mr. Williams that he was going to inspect the old zoo.

The old zoo was two miles from the main zoo and was being used for a holding compound. Built in 1937, it was rustic and all the trees were fully grown. Because the zoo public was not allowed to see it any longer, the landscaping had been allowed to become overgrown. The tight little canyon surrounding the old zoo was dark and eerie. Sounds were magnified, giving the illusion that anything you heard was right next to you. You knew as soon as you entered the gate that you were on your own. If you were attacked by a man or beast, there would be no help for a long while. Entering was always a little act of bravery.

When Hans entered the old Griffith Park Zoo, he patted his revolver to make sure he had a good sense of its location. He left the vehicle and loosed the chain holding the gate fast. Fog swirled around the headlights of the security vehicle and created a mystical atmosphere. Hans was uneasy. Adrenaline was surging through his veins, and his heart was pounding for no reason that he could discern. He drove his vehicle just inside the gate and got out of the car to replace the chain. He had the eerie feeling that he was being watched, and he was right.

Susie, a petite, six-year-old chimp, stared into the night where the fog was aglow. She heard the whirring of the car engine. It was a familiar sound, one that she heard four times nightly. She shouldn't have been seeing the glow of the headlights, but she had escaped earlier that evening and was out for a walk in the fog-shrouded old zoo. She stared with interest as the headlights drew near. She liked people, and a little company would be fine. None of the other chimps had joined her. She had been thoughtful enough to close the cage door behind her, although she had left the back door to her exhibit open. From where she was standing, she could vaguely see Hans getting out of the car. The light inside the car stayed on, and she walked towards it as Hans walked away from it. When she got to the car, Hans was several yards away checking the locks on the cage doors.

Susie saw the gun on the front seat and became uncomfortable. All the chimps recognized guns; they knew well the guns with painful tranquilizer darts that were used on them each year before their physical exams. She decided that she didn't want to be anywhere near the gun, so she set out to find Hans for a little companionship.

Hans had just discovered the open back door of her exhibit. He entered slowly to see if anything was out of order. Since he didn't remember the number of chimpanzees in the collection, he didn't realize that one was missing. He smiled as he recorded in his notebook that the door had been left open. He didn't like Elvin Rayburn, their keeper, and was glad to report that he had fouled up. He tucked his black steel flashlight under his chin and pulled out his notebook and a pen. While he was making his notes, Susie walked up silently behind him and patted his leg to greet him.

His reaction could not have been more dramatic if it had been a Middle Eastern terrorist. He threw himself against the wall of the exhibit and dropped his flashlight, breaking the bulb. As it fell, he caught a glimpse of Susie running away. He had screamed so loud that she could only believe something dangerous was about to happen. She wasn't going to stay there and face it either. No, sir. She would run and hide until it was safe.

The thought of being that close to an ape catapulted Hans toward the car. He fell twice scrambling through the darkness, guided only by the glow of the headlights and the sound of the engine. He was hyperventilating and nearly fainted as he threw himself into the car and slammed the door. He lay back in the seat waiting for his heart to stop pounding. He didn't want to sound terrified when he called the main zoo to announce the emergency.

"Security Two to Security One, come in please."

"Security Two, go ahead please."

"We have an ape of some sort out over here. What should I do? Over."

"Standby, Security Two, while I find out."

The young security guard at the main zoo looked at the policy manual under escaped animals and saw that there were five numbers to call. He chose Dr. Hart because he was the most approachable. Although he was a world-renowned scholar in his field, Dr. Hart seemed always to have the time and the inclination to be friendly. The vast majority of the zoo staff would have died for him without being asked. He was, and still is, a great man.

Dr. Hart had gone to bed early that night and was asleep when the security guard called. Mrs. Hart answered the phone and had to wake her husband from a deep sleep to come to the phone.

"Hart here," the vet said, rubbing his eyes and trying to get a grip on reality.

"Doc, we got an ape loose at the old zoo. What do we do?"

"That would be a chimp. Could be real dangerous if it got out of the zoo into residential Griffith Park. Chimps could do some real damage. They can be dangerous. Do anything you can to keep it from getting out of the zoo." Dr. Hart was still waking up and more thinking out loud than giving orders. "I'll be there in 20 minutes. Call Ed and Tony and tell them to meet me at the old zoo."

"Sure, Doc, anything you say."

When Dr. Hart began to wake up, he wondered which security guard was working patrol that night. He was hoping that it wasn't Hans because he knew Hans would blow everything out of proportion. Well, he'd be there in 20 minutes and not much could happen in that time. He finished dressing, jumped in his MG, and headed for the zoo at top speed.

"Security Two to Security One, help's on the way. Hart says you got a loose chimp over there and that they can be real dangerous. He says we can't let it get out of the zoo because if it got to the homes, it could do some real damage, maybe hurt someone real good. I don't know what to tell you to do but that's what he said."

Hans put his hand on his revolver and replied, "I'll do everything I can."

He stared into the fog. Holding his revolver gave him a sense of power and confidence. He pulled it out of his holster and held it in his lap for several seconds. He then stepped out of the car and stared into the night, searching the shadows for some evidence of the escaped chimp. He couldn't see her, but she could see him.

Susie watched as Hans looked in all directions. He wasn't screaming anymore, so the danger must have passed. She began cautiously walking toward Hans.

The more Dr. Hart thought about what he had said the more he wished he had not painted such a dangerous picture of the chimps. He wished he had just waited until he got there to take care of it himself. Finally, he made the turnoff to the zoo and sped past the security office to pick up the tranquilizer gun and his black bag.

Meanwhile, Hans saw movement in the lights in front of the car. It was Susie. His heart began to pound. He may as well have had a lion stalking him. Remembering the warning he had been given, he judged that Susie was acting aggressively by approaching him at all. He slowly lifted his revolver and pointed it at her chest.

Susie looked up at Hans. The headlights were blinding her, but she could see that he was pointing something at her. She slowed her approach. When she was about ten feet away, she could see that he was pointing a gun at her. Terrified, she ran into the night as Hans pulled the trigger.

Dr. Hart pulled up to the old zoo gate, quickly threw the gate open, and drove in without bothering to shut the gate behind him. He could see the glowing lights of the security vehicle. Skidding to a halt next to it, he jumped from the car.

Hans greeted him with a satisfied look on his face. "Emergency's over, Dr. Hart. The ape tried to charge me, and I had to shoot it."

"What? Where is it, quick? Take me to it," Dr. Hart begged.

Hans led him just ten feet to where Susie lay face down in the leaves and dirt. The doctor dove for her, lifted her up, and moved her into the lights of the vehicle. She was limp in his arms. He carefully laid her down and pressed his ear to her chest. There was no heartbeat or pulse or reflexes. She was dead, and there would be no bringing her back.

Dr. Hart began to sob. He held Susie in his lap and rocked her back and forth as though she were a child, his child.

Hans, confused, asked, "Did I do wrong?"

Dr. Hart looked up with tear-filled eyes and replied, "Hans, this was Susie. She used to be a pet. She was the tamest chimp in the collection. I set you up to kill the tamest chimp in our collection. This is my fault."

"It looked like she was charging me. I was just protecting myself."

"She was probably trying to make friends, Hans, but you wouldn't have known because I told you guys how dangerous our chimps were. It's not your fault."

The other keepers arrived in time to see Dr. Hart gently lay the chimp in his car so that he might take her to the main zoo. He was teary, and no one spoke because they didn't know what to say. Dr. Hart stayed several hours that night because he decided to perform her necropsy to determine exactly why she had died. What he discovered bothered him a great deal, but he didn't know what to do with the information. The chimp had not been shot in the chest as Hans had claimed, but in the back. She must have thought Hans was holding a tranquilizer gun, and she was running away from it when he shot. Hans had not wanted her to get out of the zoo. Dr. Hart felt worse than ever. He knew that somehow his directions had inspired this moment, and he knew that no one would want to believe it. They would want to believe that Hans was a gun-happy jerk and blame the whole mess on him.

That's exactly what happened. The harder Dr. Hart tried to accept the blame for what had happened, the more the zoo personnel sought to exonerate him and blame Hans. They would say, "Isn't it just like Hart to take the blame for someone? Well, we know that gun-happy Kraut was the real criminal." No matter where Hans went after that, keepers would turn their backs to him or pretend to shoot him with their fingers. They called him names like Chimp-killer.

Hans would try to smile, but it was plain that he felt more alone than ever. He spent more time at the health center because we were kind to him. His visits were temporary sanctuary from the cruel storm that assailed him when he drove through the rest of the zoo.

The keepers never really let go of the event. After they added Susie's death to Hans's prejudice and isolationist policies, they made him a social outcast, an untouchable.

I was frustrated by the situation. Hans needed to be loved as much as any man I have ever known, but a disastrous moment now made that an unlikely possibility. I didn't like what he had done, but when I put myself in his position I could not say for sure that I would not have done the same thing.

- He had been working under very stressful conditions at night. The zoo is a frightening place at night.
- Hans didn't know one chimp from another. It wasn't his job. Some of the chimps, especially Jeanie and Toto, would have been unpredictably dangerous.
- The information by which Hans made his decisions had been given by a reliable man, a world authority. He had said chimps were dangerous and ought not to be allowed to leave the zoo.

- The zoo didn't allow their security force to carry guns, but Hans had a license and as a private citizen was within his rights. (After that incident a written policy was issued forbidding the security force to carry arms. It was too late for Susie, but no animal has been killed since that time.)
- The security guards were never trained to handle animal-related emergencies.

This incident truly represented the zoo's worst night. Nothing so unjust or frustrating has occurred since at the zoo.

I hate to think about that night. To relive it frustrates me. It does illustrate the reality of this present age, some of what is and has been true since the fall. Life is full of confusion. Life isn't fair. Misunderstandings abound, and death is all around us. These were the consequences when Adam and Eve chose to be the god of their own lives.

Thanks be to God there is coming a time when we will all be changed. It will only take a second. We will be changed as quickly as an eye blinks. This will happen when the last trumpet sounds. The dead will be raised to live forever. And we will all be changed (*see* 1 Corinthians 15:51-52).

We are going to be made perfect, and so will our circumstances. There will be no more tears, no more injustice or confusion—only joy at God's right hand forevermore. Sound too good to be true? You can believe it.

God has promised that our sorrows won't go on forever. They will have an end. God wants us to know this; He has given us many Scriptures that convey this truth. If you are now going through some industrial-strength sadness, read the following passages. They should encourage you.

> Gladness and joy will overtake them, and sorrow and sighing will flee away (Isaiah 35:10 NIV).
>
> Your sun shall no more go down, nor your moon withdraw itself; for the Lord will be your everlasting

> light, and your days of mourning shall be ended (Isaiah 60:20).
>
> Their life shall be like a watered garden, and they shall languish no more. . . . I will turn their mourning into joy, I will comfort them (Jeremiah 31:12-13).
>
> Though he cause grief, he will have compassion according to the abundance of his steadfast love (Lamentations 3:32).
>
> Truly, truly, I say to you . . . you will be sorrowful, but your sorrow will turn to joy (John 16:20).

Indeed, God promises to heal our grief and sorrow. And we can take heart in the truth shared by Paul in 2 Corinthians 4:16-18:

> Though outwardly we are wasting away, yet inwardly we are being renewed day by day. For our light and momentary troubles are achieving for us an eternal glory that far outweighs them all. So we fix our eyes not on what is seen, but on what is unseen. For what is seen is temporary, but what is unseen is eternal.

Chapter Twenty-Six

The Gelada Named Barnaby

Baboons are really wonderful animals. They are large and formidable monkeys. They will climb trees but live most of their lives on the ground. There are eight species of baboons, each one bold and stunning in its own way. They are family oriented, living in troops of 12 to 50 animals. They walk together like an army, with one general and a couple of sergeants in the middle of the troop. The mothers with young babies accompany them in the center. On the perimeters are the young males, and just one step toward the center the adult females without young.

The general stays at the center because it is equidistant to whatever danger might appear. Should a leopard or hyena or even another troop of baboons arrive, he is off in a flash to defend his troop. They can be savage, but left undisturbed, they are gentle, orderly animals.

Our zoo at one time or another exhibited five of the eight species. This story is about one of the most impressive of the species, the Gelada. The Gelada baboon comes from

Ethiopia and lives above the 1,800-foot level in the foothills of mountains. They eat fruits, vegetables, and animals when they can catch them. They are a luxurious dark brown, and the males have the most spectacular long coats of any of the species. Their coat could even be referred to as a mane.

We had nine Geladas in the collection until Barnaby, a teenage male, darted past a keeper who was not careful when leaving Barnaby's cage. As social as baboons are, no one believed that this was any big deal. Everyone knew that Barnaby would hang around, and when he got hungry, he could be trapped. A few grapes in a live trap, and, bingo, Barnaby would be home again and back with his family. Everyone but Barnaby knew this.

Barnaby was different. You see, there are always exceptions. Just about the time you think you have an animal figured out, boom, you're in for a surprise.

Barnaby, by human years, would have been about 13. He was not yet half grown but full of spunk and very independent. He was also intelligent. When the trap was set up near his cage, he would not go near it. He knew what it was and steered clear despite the fact that he was hungry and wanted the food that was in the trap. His cage was not far from the back fence of the zoo, and in the early morning hours he began to leave to go exploring.

The zoo is located in Griffith Park, and Griffith Park adjoins the Hollywood Hills. The zoo is in the midst of thousands of acres of wilderness full of wild animals and patroled by park rangers. The kicker is that this postage stamp of wilderness is surrounded by one of the world's largest cities. This undeveloped area is covered largely by the brush that typically covers the foothills in Southern California, and the shady canyon areas are made up of oak woodlands. Oddly enough, the area was ideal for Barnaby and not unlike his native habitat in Ethiopia.

Barnaby began to lose a little weight. Those who would see him visit his family made note that his ribs were showing, and some of us were afraid that he might die of malnutrition. But food was our only bait, so he was not fed outside the cage.

His journeys from the zoo became lengthened as hunger drove him into a survival mode. On one of his journeys, he found a spring. Near the spring he found blackberries. Barnaby feasted on the berries, and, for the first time in a long time, he was full when he slept that night.

Days turned into weeks, and the keepers noted that they were seeing Barnaby less frequently. His journeys for food were taking him farther and farther from the zoo, and he was finding a wider range of things he could eat. When he could catch them, he ate locusts and grasshoppers. He also ate lizards. He was trying a variety of leaves and seeds and discovering weekly that there was food everywhere. The weight loss stopped. Barnaby was breaking even until he made a terrific discovery.

One day the brush ended abruptly, and green lawns were everywhere. So were people, so he stayed at the edge of the picnic grounds for fear of being caught.

One morning at about 11:30, Barnaby went to visit the picnic area. He came out of the brush face to face with a five-year-old boy eating a peanut butter and jelly sandwich. The boy was fascinated by Barnaby and laughed at him. When the little boy laughed, he showed Barnaby his teeth and opened his mouth. In baboon, this is a challenge to fight, and Barnaby felt discomfort. He was not yet old enough that he would attack, but he knew what the boy's actions meant. The little boy also stared at him, which was not considered to be polite among baboons.

Then this boy did the strangest thing. He threw his sandwich to Barnaby and made sounds that sounded soothing. He was saying, "Nice monkey," but to Barnaby, it was just soothing, no more. Barnaby picked up the sandwich. It smelled good. He licked it, and it tasted good, so he took a bite. This was a turning point in Barnaby's existence. This was when he crossed the line from survival to abundance. Barnaby discovered that everybody wanted to feed him. He was so full on some days that he turned down food. He was now approaching people and taking the food from their hands. He was still young, so no one felt threatened by his appearance. Barnaby, by nature, was gentle, unlike his militant father Ho Chi Minh. But he was passing through adolescence quickly. He was approaching 40 pounds and could eventually weigh 100 pounds.

One evening after Barnaby had entertained the picnickers and stuffed himself, he had a very close call. He was on his way back to the zoo, where he would visit his mother and extended family and probably sleep. Unknowingly, he passed under a tree from which a female mountain lion was surveying the area for something to eat. She had had two bad days of hunting and was both cranky and hungry. When the predator saw Barnaby she was startled. Her instincts and experience did not prepare her for attacking a baboon outright so she did not leap. She decided to follow Barnaby, now feeling that he looked enough like prey to consider the possibilities. If he had been full grown, Barnaby would have been more than a match for an adult female mountain lion, but at 50 pounds he was in trouble.

Barnaby felt uneasy. He didn't know why, but something was wrong. He wasn't hearing enough bird song. The other animals were bothered, and he knew it. The female lioness was downwind, so Barnaby didn't catch her scent. Stealth was her middle name, so he didn't hear her. Still he knew something was up, so he quickened his pace. She picked up her pace also and began to close in on the resourceful young baboon.

The mountain lion snapped a twig and Barnaby heard it. Adrenaline surged through his system as he took flight. The mountain lion heard Barnaby run, and she made an all-out effort to catch him. Barnaby looked back and saw her closing the gap. He leapt into an oak tree and began to climb.

His heart began to pound harder when he discovered that she, too, could climb, and nearly as well as he. He was 30 feet up into the branches and realized that she was still closing in. When she was within five feet, he threw himself to lower branches and fell to the ground. She leapt too, but, thinking better of a blind fall through the branches to the ground, she grabbed a branch and hung on for a second until she was able to pull herself back into the tree.

Barnaby wasted no time. He ran straight to the zoo fence, which he climbed faster than he had ever done before. It was a close call, and he hoped he would never see the lion again. He slept fitfully that night and dreamed he was being chased by the female lioness. He leaned against the wire, holding his mother's arm while he slept.

Barnaby was beginning to miss being with his kind. His existence was lonely. Weeks had turned into months, and he was becoming an adult male. He was now 75 pounds. He also had a very strong desire to mate. But look though he might, there were no baboons in the park. There were nights when he would reach through the chain-link fencing to groom his mother. He was still attached to her, and her touch was reassuring.

When Barnaby reached 90 pounds and his mane became luxurious, the picnickers began to realize that their children could be at risk. They began to report Barnaby to the park rangers, who in turn called the zoo and asked us to step up efforts to recapture the baboon that had been out for more than a year now.

Meetings were held, and it was decided that Dr. Wordsworth would set up a blind and hide there like a duck hunter. He would simply wait until Barnaby came down to be with his family and dart him with the tranquilizer gun. The task wouldn't be too hard to carry out because Barnaby had established a predictable schedule. He usually came into the zoo about 7:00 P.M. during daylight savings time. It was decided that security should watch for Barnaby's entry into the zoo and see just how predictable he was. It was as if he had a Rolex; he walked across the road that led to his family every night between 7:02 and 7:04.

Barnaby's last week of freedom prepared him for recapture. On Sunday night of that week, he was taking a long drink at the spring when the female lioness showed up again. Barnaby was afraid, but not as afraid as he had been at their last meeting. She didn't look as large to him as she had looked before, and of course he had gained 60 pounds. His canines had grown a full inch and were longer than hers. They stared at each other for several seconds, each waiting to see what the other would do. She growled in a threatening way, and Barnaby's hair stood on end not because he was afraid but because he wished to threaten back. He pulled back his lips and exposed his canines. Then he lurched forward and barked as baboons do when they want to appear aggressive.

The predator knew she was no longer a match for the now-adult male baboon, so she hissed and gave ground. After she had backed up about five feet she walked away, looking back just once to hiss. Barnaby never saw her again.

The next Tuesday Barnaby ran into a mated pair of coyotes that had just killed a brush-tailed rabbit. Barnaby loved fresh rabbit so he advanced. He barked and threatened, but the coyotes would not back away from their prey. Barnaby charged, but the coyotes crouched and held their ground. If there had been one coyote, Barnaby would have simply attacked and taken the rabbit, but there were two. It was a standoff until a long-submerged instinct surfaced. Barnaby picked up a large rock and threw it at the coyote nearest to him. It hit her in the muzzle, and she yelped. Barnaby found another rock and hit her again. She backed up, but the male stood firm over the rabbit. Barnaby found a large branch with dead leaves and ran at the male, swinging the branch back and forth and making a lot of noise as the branch hit nearby bushes. That did it for Mr. and Mrs. Coyote. They ran and didn't look back.

Barnaby picked up the rabbit and enjoyed it immensely. He peeled it as one would peel an orange. Then he savored his meal.

On Wednesday of that same week, Barnaby reached into a bush to pick up a seed pod and was nearly bitten by a rattlesnake. It frightened him quite badly, and he was jumpy and irritable for the rest of the day.

During one morning Barnaby grew a bit impatient when a woman in the park kept withdrawing her offer to give him a piece of apple, so he barked at her and simply yanked the apple away from her. He had no intention of biting her; he just wasn't in the mood for games. But when the lady reported the incident to the park ranger, she made it sound as though Barnaby had been aggressive and threatening.

The ranger let the zoo know in no uncertain terms that they had better capture Barnaby soon or plan a funeral for him. The zoo assured the ranger that a plan was in effect and Barnaby would be home soon.

On Friday evening, Dr. Wordsworth carefully prepared a capture dart and loaded it in the rifle. He leaned the rifle against a wall. Then he placed some grapes and bananas in a pile in the middle of the road, about 40 feet from the blind where he would be hiding when he attempted his shot.

Dr. Wordsworth entered the blind at 6:30 P.M. anticipating Barnaby's arrival. It was daylight savings time, and there was plenty of light and would continue to be until about 8:00 P.M. He stuck the rifle barrel through the viewing slot and kept it aimed near the bananas and grapes.

The evening was beautiful, and Dr. Wordsworth was feeling like the proverbial great white hunter. He was in a lot of shrubbery, and the zoo was full of animals making territorial sounds. The gibbons were hooting, the macaws were screeching, and the lions were providing the bass line to the wild symphony of sounds that filled the valley in which the zoo was nestled.

As it neared 7:00 P.M. the doctor tensed and waited anxiously for Barnaby to show. He was not disappointed. At

7:02 P.M. Barnaby's inner biological clock prompted him to return to the zoo.

He walked up to the grapes and bananas with suspicion. They had never been there before, and he wondered why now. He looked carefully in every direction but saw nothing at all out of the ordinary. He walked around the food and bent over to smell it. As he did so, his hindquarters moved into the doctor's gun sight.

The blast of the rifle startled Barnaby, and he ran for the back fence. In seconds he was aware of a sharp stinging sensation and stopped to pull the dart out of his leg. He then cleared the first fence, crossed a walking path, and threw himself into the bison yard. His heart was pounding, moving the tranquilizer through his system at a rapid pace. By the time he cleared the bison exhibit, he had just the perimeter fence to jump. He would then be in the wild and free.

But Barnaby started feeling foggy. The world began turning about him. He reached for the fence, but he couldn't remember why. So he sat down next to it as he watched everything grow dim and roll about like a storm-tossed sea. He saw several animal keepers rushing to him, but he was not afraid, for the drug had taken effect. Nothing really mattered at all; everything went black.

When Barnaby woke up, he was in a fairly large cage at the health center. He had been given a thorough physical examination. Pending any negative results in his blood tests, throat cultures, and the investigation for internal parasites, he would be reunited with his family after 18 months in the wild.

The tests only confirmed what we could already see. Barnaby was one of the finest specimens of adult male Gelada baboons in captivity. He was reunited with his family, and his loneliness was cured. Although Barnaby had been mellow in the wild, he became very dominant in captivity. He displaced his father and became the father of dozens of babies himself. He stayed at the top for several years but then was replaced by a male that weighed 40 pounds more than Barnaby ever did in his prime.

• • •

Barnaby's story is wonderful because it so illustrates God's provision for His creatures. The means to survive were always there, but it took Barnaby a while to discover that. He was lean until he began to avail himself of all there was to choose from. Barnaby found that there was more than enough food available for him to survive. So it wasn't a question of survival, but of how abundantly he wanted to live.

One of the Lord Jesus Christ's purposes for coming to earth is expressed in the Gospel of John: "I came that they may have life, and have it abundantly" (John 10:10). Elsewhere, Jesus said,

> Do not worry about your life, what you will eat or drink; or about your body, what you will wear. Is not life more important than food, and the body more important than clothes? Look at the birds of the air; they do not sow or reap or store away in barns, and yet your heavenly Father feeds them. Are you not much more valuable than they? Who of you by worrying can add a single hour to his life?
>
> And why do you worry about clothes? See how the lilies of the field grow. They do not labor or spin. Yet I tell you that not even Solomon in all his splendor was dressed like one of these. If that is how God clothes the grass of the field, which is here today and tomorrow is thrown into the fire, will he not much more clothe you, O you of little faith? So do not worry, saying, "What shall we eat?" or "What shall we drink?" or "What shall we wear?" For the pagans run after all these things, and your heavenly Father knows that you need

> them. But seek first his kingdom and his righteousness, and all these things will be given to you as well. Therefore do not worry about tomorrow, for tomorrow will worry about itself. Each day has enough trouble of its own (Matthew 6:25-34 NIV).

A sad truth concerning our human nature is that we are often satisfied far less than God has intended. It may be interesting for you to know that to this day the nation of Israel, God's people, has never claimed anywhere near the amount of land God offered them.

And so it is with us. Far too soon we become satisfied . . . and end up missing the best part of the banquet.

Chapter Twenty-seven

Mosquitoes and Flies

It is both comforting and disturbing to know that God created everything for a specific purpose. Nothing was an accident; nothing was unplanned. Not one of the 4.4 million creatures that fly, walk, swim, crawl, wriggle, slide, or hop the earth was a joke or an afterthought. Everything does something that makes its own existence worthwhile. Each creature performs a foreordained function that benefits nature and glorifies God.

In Ecclesiastes 3:14 we read, "I know that whatever God does endures for ever; nothing can be added to it, nor anything taken from it." When God created the earth and all of the animals, it was complete. Moreover, He said that everything was good. But many Christians I have met don't share that view. They want to apologize for some of God's most amazing inventions—His animals. Even worse, they take delight in stepping on them, shooting them, running over them, and swatting them until each spark of life is extinguished.

I am referring to a host of vermin that man finds repulsive: spiders, snakes, roaches, rats, mosquitoes, and flies, to name a few. The average middle-class Christian is quietly embarrassed about these creations and would gladly let the devil take credit for them if they could. Well, it's time that someone took up their defense and made sure that God received the glory for the great things that He has done. I mean to include all the aforementioned creatures in my defense. On the day that God made them He declared that they were good. The Scriptures make it clear that what God has declared to be good we have no business declaring evil.

Perhaps we fear these creatures because we tend to fear what we least understand. The creature that we most understand is man, so when we see creatures that do not remind us of our species we are repulsed. We are afraid of snakes and spiders because they do not look like us. Snakes don't have enough arms and legs to remind us of men, and spiders have too many.

On the other hand, we are attracted to species that do resemble man. Go to your local Hallmark store and make a note of what animals you see on greeting cards. You will find primates first (monkeys and apes) and then bears. Psychologists have known about man's attraction to these creatures for years, and the greeting-card companies have taken advantage of psychological knowledge to make a profit. With the exception of butterflies, when have you seen a greeting card with an insect of some kind, such as a spider? If you do, it's sure to be a cartoon insect that has been made to look like a caricature of a human. Check this out for yourself next time you're at the store.

Fear is the basis of our revulsion. And we hate what we fear.

On many occasions I have asked people the question, "Why do you think God made mosquitoes and flies?" The answer is usually self-centered. People, even the educated, say it was to punish and harass sinful man. It has rarely occurred to anyone that these two amazing creatures do us far more good than harm. "No!" you say? "Yes!" I answer emphatically.

"How?" you respond. I'm so glad you asked. Let me tell you how in a story—not a fictional story exactly, but fiction based entirely on the real world. In fact, this story is unfolding somewhere on the earth as it is written and again as you are reading it.

Tonda the white-tailed deer stood proudly in the afternoon sun and watched over the small herd of females that followed him from feeding ground to feeding ground. These deer were of a species known as browsers. This means that they ate leaves. It was spring now, and the trees at the base of the mountain were beginning to bud, forming new leaves soft and sweet. The herd was glad, for they were tired of the dry leaves they had survived on during the winter.

The new leaves were forming in the valley where Tonda led his herd, but not in the mountains where the snow was just now beginning to melt. The spring rains had formed pools and ponds in the lower valleys, and the warming trend had awakened the insects that had slept all winter.

Diptera, a female mosquito, had mated with a chance male and eggs had begun to form inside her. Her instincts told her she must have blood or her young would not be strong and healthy. The nectar that her species normally drinks is low in the protein necessary to form her eggs. So she, along with thousands of her kind, began to seek out animals that they could pierce in order to obtain the blood that the young needed to survive. Only the female mosquitoes bite people, and only then for the good of their young.

As the sun was setting, Diptera found Tonda and settled near his eye. She landed so softly Tonda had no idea that he was being visited. She pierced his flesh and injected a small amount of saliva. The saliva created an irritation that caused swelling, signaling the body to send more blood to repair the area. Diptera was bloating on blood even before Tonda began to itch. He rubbed his nose against the lower branch of the black oak whose tender young leaves he was devouring with relish. Diptera flew away just before she would have been crushed by the movement.

She flew until she smelled water and landed at the edge of a small pond. She lowered her abdomen into the pond and laid several dozen eggs. When she finished, she left to feed on the nectar she would find at the center of the tiny flowers beginning to herald spring.

Diptera was the first to bite Tonda that night but not the last. He was bitten about 50 times by other expectant mothers who were seeking out protein for their young. Tonda knew instinctively that it was time to begin climbing the mountain. The higher he would go the fewer the mosquitoes. So he walked up the hillside until the night air had just a bit of a bite to it. Here the mosquitoes would continue to sleep for five or six more days. Tonda browsed again, free of the annoying mosquitoes' bites.

In the valley Diptera wriggled deep into the bloom of a small purple flower and sipped a bit of nectar. As she sipped, a bit of pollen stuck to her body. It rubbed off in the next bloom, giving the next plant the power to make seeds. Diptera and her species actually pollinate as many flowers as bees but are rarely given credit for their efforts.

Tonda discovered seven days later that the mosquitoes were again at work. So he moved up again. As he moved, the herd pruned the lower branches of the trees on which they fed, allowing light to penetrate to the new growth of grasses and plants near the base of the trees. The herd also fertilized as they went. Now spring was moving them higher and higher to be relieved of the insatiable appetites of the mosquitoes.

By late spring the snows were all but melted, and the deer had reached the highest elevation. Millions of mosquitoes clambered for blood as summer set in. They fought to reach small pools and ponds, and even at 10,000 feet the deer were harassed by the tiny marauders. Tonda's instincts told him that they needed to return to lower elevations, where the pools had now dried up. There they would again find relief—at least the numbers would be significantly less.

In the valley below, Diptera was again heading for a small lake where she could deposit her eggs. A violet-green swallow hunting for small insects saw her, swooped down, and in a second captured the mosquito. She was fed to the swallow's young that evening, and even the small drop of blood Diptera had extracted from a rabbit was not wasted. The young swallow enjoyed it immensely as his mother filled his crop.

Summer then gave way to fall. Now Tonda and his herd again felt the bite of cooler nights and the boredom of falling leaves. The moderate climate of the valley beckoned them, so down they came.

Late one afternoon the herd was surprised by a mountain lion. The does and now older fawns ran for their lives, but Tonda, with his awesome rack of antlers, stayed to fight. Because of a powerful hunger, the mountain lion decided to brave the powerful buck. Tonda held his ground while the cat looked for an opening. As it charged, Tonda lowered his head and drove his antlers deep into the predator's chest. It turned out to be a fatal encounter for the mountain lion, but before it died it sank its fangs deep into the shoulder of the brave stag.

Tonda stood panting over the dead cat and felt the stabbing pain from the wound in his shoulder. He turned and limped his way down the hill to join his herd once again.

In the morning Tonda was awakened by the buzzing of flies around the wound. Many had dined on the dried blood and had recognized that the wound would be an excellent place to lay their eggs. The eggs soon hatched, and their larvae (maggots) began to eat the dead and decaying flesh in and around the wound. God ordained that maggots eat only dead and decaying flesh. Consequently the new growth was kept free from infection, and the two-inch wound was allowed to heal from the inside out. Had the flies never found

Tonda, he would surely have died, for the bite of any cat is very nasty and apt to infect.

This wasn't the first time flies had saved his life. When he was a young buck, he had fought for and lost the right to run with the females. He had gotten four deep wounds from Dovar the mighty buck. The flies had come at that time, too, and cleaned his wounds, allowing him to live. Flies clean all dead and decaying things. They consume and eliminate, and plants absorb the flies' waste for food. Flies live but six weeks and are themselves food for many animals. Those that are not eaten leave their bodies to the earth for plant food. These plants, in turn, take in what we breathe out and give us oxygen in return.

So it was that Tonda returned to the valley, having served the forest while ascending and descending the mountain. The mosquito was his herdsman and the fly his doctor. The mosquito also helped the plants to seed, and the fly helped the plants to feed.

• • •

Made to harass man, you say? I hope you do not say so anymore. Up until 1932 maggots were still being used by human doctors to do the same things for people that they do for deer. There are few humans alive whose ancestors were not saved by maggots after having been bitten by a beast or pierced by a sword. In fact, if you are badly burned, your doctor will probably ask you to allow him to introduce maggots to your wounds. They will remove the dead tissue more skillfully than could any human surgeon.

Of the millions of animals God created, none was made without a purpose. Each animal was distinctly designed to perform some task that would benefit nature or the creation. Even the animals that we hate perform valuable functions. Man, however, was created with no ecological purpose, and yet we were created with the most valuable purpose of all.

Although we fill no ecological niche, we have the opportunity to glorify God and enjoy Him forever, as stated in the Westminster Catechism.

Do you still want to give Satan credit for mosquitoes and flies? He couldn't even make gnats.

CHAPTER TWENTY-EIGHT

Keep Your Head Above Water

Henry was a sloth bear. Now describing a sloth bear is no simple task, but if you can imagine a bear made out of assorted spare bear parts, you might start to get the picture.

Sloth bears are on the small side, weighing not more than 200 pounds. They are bushy all over, particularly around the head. When you look at a sloth bear, you might feel reluctant to ascribe its origin to one of the six days of Creation. Once you've seen one, you might think that way back at the beginning of time a black male lion had married a small female bear. (Maybe the lion had poor eyesight and the she-bear never bothered to mention that she was a bear.)

Sloth bears are mostly black, with just a touch of white or gray around their muzzles, but that mostly depends on their age. Tufts of hair stick up from the ends of their saggy ears. And they are pigeon-toed; they rock back and forth when they walk.

Henry was a prime specimen of sloth bear, but he was also a little more than that. Henry's behavior was as bizarre as bears get. He had several quirks that made him memorable. To give you some idea of how special Henry was, consider this. The zoo owned 16 bears that represented six different species, but only two were named: Ivan, the 950-pound polar bear, and little Henry, the eccentric sloth bear.

Henry was known for his temper tantrums. He threw them all the time, and he didn't require much of a reason. Flies buzzing around his head might set him off. Being denied a treat after he had begged for food might do it. Being let in for dinner two minutes late was a sure bet.

You've probably heard the expression, "You're acting like a real bear." The first time they used it, they put Henry's picture next to it—not a full body shot, but a close-up of his face. It made you wonder why they named him Henry, unless he was named for Henry VIII. I would have chosen the name Grumpy.

As grouchy as Henry was, you couldn't help but like the little fellow because he was possessed of the same mettle as Snow White's Grumpy. I saw him as stouthearted and brave, and it hurts to tell you his story.

Henry's bear moat was constructed below the level of the surrounding drainage system. When water ran into the moat or the surrounding drains they would begin to fill until a float activated a pump that would drain the excess water away. The drains had always worked faithfully, and it never occurred to anyone that one night they would not.

During one unusually rainy January, the ground became fully saturated and torrents of water were cascading down through the terrain as the rain challenged the hillsides with relentless fury. The pumps had to work overtime for several days in a row, and we didn't know it but their strength was failing. Their time was silently at hand.

The night before the pumps failed was like any other. When Henry's keeper, George, left to go home he smiled at Henry, who had just come off exhibit and was already busy sifting through a pile of delicacies that George had lovingly prepared minutes before. Henry didn't look up when George said good night. It wasn't his way. But this was always the one moment each day when Henry was incapable of hiding his capacity for joy. He loved food, and he didn't care who knew it. The last sounds George heard as he closed the back door of the bear grotto were Henry's ecstatic utterances, spontaneously generated while eating his favorite foods.

After George left, Henry ate and ate until his floor was completely free of any small tidbits of food. He then licked his paws clean and circled his grotto until he was ready to lie down for the night. Sleep came quickly to a mind with no cares. In no time Henry was snoring and dreaming of more treats and faraway Eastern jungles with exotic vines and flowers.

Henry was completely unaware that the pumps had broken and that the water in his moat was rising at an alarming rate. He did not realize that before morning his grotto could be his tomb. He was surrounded by concrete and steel, and there was no way of escape.

It wasn't until 3:00 in the morning that Henry was awakened by water that was licking at his right paw, which was dangling from his sleeping platform. He stood and viewed something he was unable to understand. His cage was filling with water. By 3:30 that morning the water had risen to his belly. Nobody was there to see it, but I'm sure Henry threw a tantrum—a first-class tizzy. He probably began by jumping up and down on his front feet. Then in full bad humor, he jumped up and down on all fours. It didn't do any good though, because the water kept rising and was now up to his neck. I believe his instincts to survive were now stimulated and he would have paced with his head high. But only minutes later Henry was beyond pacing. He was forced to do what all bears can do so well—stand up. Yet bears can't do this for very long; it just isn't comfortable. But for Henry, comfort was no longer an option. It was stand or die, and the water was still rising.

The only light in the bear grotto was a 25-watt bulb mounted near the ceiling. It cast an eerie light that danced dimly across the water to Henry. Henry looked at the back door, which was now four feet deep in water, and wished that George would come through and let him out on exhibit where he could crawl to higher ground. It was now 4:30 in the morning and it would be nearly four more hours before keepers began to arrive at the zoo to check on their animals. Henry didn't have that much time. The water was now up to his mouth, and he was standing on his tiptoes to breathe.

Henry continued to watch the door for George's appearance and moaned sadly because he was afraid. Being a tropical bear, he was not enjoying the cold water that engulfed him. Minutes must have seemed like hours to this frightened little sloth bear. The water was rising even more, and Henry had to dance to keep his head above water. The rain kept coming, and there was no evidence it would stop. The gully where Henry lived turned into a small lake, even outside the grotto. Security knew the tunnel leading to Henry's area was filling up with water, but it did not occur to them that the bear moat was also filling up. No emergency plan was put into action; security thought that maintenance could deal with a plugged drain later that day.

When George arrived at the zoo later that morning, he frowned at the perilous gray sky and pulled his rain gear closer to his body as he got out of his car. The rain was coming down harder than ever and stung his face and hands as he walked toward his section. He stopped to chat with Bob Morris, the aquatics keeper, who asked if maybe it was time to start thinking about building an ark. George said he didn't think that was such a far-out idea in light of the number of days in a row that it had rained. They exchanged small talk; then George walked briskly to his section. When he got to the tunnel and saw that it was waist deep in water, George's heart began to pound. Panic-stricken, he yelled "Henry!" and waded through the deep water to the bear moat.

A feeling of hopelessness overwhelmed George when he saw the lake that surrounded the bear moat. It was deep, and in George's mind, Henry was history. George plunged through the icy water and made his way to the back door of the moat. He reached under the water, opened the door, and waded inside. The 25-watt bulb, still working, offered dim light. As George's eyes adjusted, he was able to see an incredible sight. There were both of Henry's paws reaching as high as they could reach, and more importantly, George could see Henry's nose, about four inches of it, sticking above the water. George was struck silent. In that silence, he could hear Henry's systematic, rhythmic breathing. It was obvious that the bear was able to breathe only through his nose. George yelled, "Henry, hang on!" then ran for a telephone.

"Security, call maintenance and tell 'em to bring every pump they have, quickly, or we're going to lose a sloth bear. His moat is filled with water. There isn't a moment to spare. Help me!"

Security got right on it, and soon several maintenance men were busy setting pumps and firing them up. Although he was shivering, George stood chest deep in water to watch his bear. He hoped Henry would survive.

George stared at Henry's nose and, after several minutes, thought maybe there was more of it showing. George was shivering violently but declined to leave his bear. He had never felt more helpless in his life. He wanted so much to open Henry's steel door and pull him to safety, but Henry would not have understood. Henry would have turned George into shredded wheat and they both would have drowned before either of them reached the back door. There are some times a person can only wait to see what will happen; this was one of those times.

Henry's feet began to slide slowly down the wall; then suddenly his nose disappeared beneath the water. George's heart began pounding. Had the rescue attempt failed so soon? Ten, fourteen, twenty seconds passed and no Henry. George began to wade toward Henry's door. He had to do something. Thirty seconds, no bear. George fumbled for his keys, and while he did Henry surfaced, coughing and sputtering. In the darkness of the grotto, Henry had struggled underwater to find higher ground. He had mercifully struggled in the right direction. He found the front of the cage, where he could stand on his concrete drinker and hold the bars. From this position he would be able to last until the water was drained. Henry shook the water from his face, eyes, and ears, and after he did he found himself staring at George, who was smiling though teary. "Silly old bear," said George as he wiped his nose and choked back a sob.

Henry continued to stare at George, his bear brain trying to sort out whether George was causing this calamity or fixing it. He ended up giving George a what-took-you-so-long look and moaned a little to show his discomfort.

The water was now draining faster, and it was clear that Henry would live to throw another tantrum. Hundreds more, maybe thousands. He lived to a ripe old age, impressive for any bear.

• • •

How about you? Do your circumstances make you feel like you're struggling just to keep your head above water? Is it so dark that you can't see an end to the trial? This is the time to dig in, hang on, and wait for a chance to get to higher ground.

We are all characters in a book, and we are all in a chapter that's being written right now—perhaps a chapter that isn't going well at all. Whatever the case, I can assure you of two great truths: This chapter will end for good or for evil and a better chapter will follow. And the really good news is that if we know Jesus, our book will have a happy ending.

If you're the kind of person who goes to the back of a book to see how the story ends, then think on these scriptures:

They who wait for the Lord shall renew their strength (Isaiah 40:31).

You will be sorrowful, but your sorrow will turn into joy (John 16:20).

No temptation has overtaken you that is not common to man. God is faithful, and he will not let you be tempted beyond your strength, but with the temptation will also provide the way of escape, that you may be able to endure it (1 Corinthians 10:13).

When we were with you, we told you beforehand that we were to suffer affliction (1 Thessalonians 3:4).

Share in suffering as a good soldier of Christ Jesus (2 Timothy 2:3).

Struggling to keep your head above water? Remember, help is on the way. God may seem slow, but He is never late!

CHAPTER TWENTY-NINE

The Best Chimp I Have Ever Known

I will never forget Charlie. As chimps go, he was the best. Charlie was the dominant chimp of our collection and well loved by any whose privilege it had been to care for him. Charlie was a peacemaker.

The Los Angeles Zoo had eight chimps that formed a cohesive group. They were tight because they had a leader who didn't put up with any monkey business. Charlie spent a good deal of time keeping his group at peace, and that was no easy assignment. There was Toto, who was a former circus chimp that stirred up trouble whenever he could. He would often hoot and scream and charge his cage mates. He would then slap them with the back of his hand and run away. Then Toto would make dramatic and threatening gestures, and that's when Charlie would swing into action.

Charlie was a little lighter than Toto but had long since established who was boss. Charlie would charge Toto and hold him down and scream at him. Toto would act submissive and Charlie would let him off the hook. In no time, Toto would be back to his old tricks, but Charlie never gave up on Toto. He tried his best, but Toto was a hopeless case.

Jeanie was no gift, either. She was always on the edge of a fit and very unpredictable. But Charlie was equal to all of his responsibilities. He was truly an exceptional chimpanzee.

One day a decision was made to remodel the very inadequate chimpanzee exhibit. It was also decided that the eight chimps would be kept at the health center until the remodeling was completed. We divided the group in half and placed them in adjacent cages. I can't remember whether there was much thought as to how we should divide them, but rational or not, our plan turned out to be a disaster.

Toto and Jeanie were housed with two of the young chimps in one cage while Charlie was housed with the coquettish Annie, the beautiful Bonnie, and the always affectionate Judy. It should have been heaven for Charlie to be separated from Toto, but that's not how it turned out.

The months began to pass, and Toto quickly realized that Charlie could do little more than yell at him from the next cage. Charlie would try his best to govern his group from the next cage, but it was futile. He started to lose a little weight and began to show signs of depression. One morning, we found that our beloved group leader had died during the night. He died sitting up, leaning against the side of the cage nearest to Toto's group.

I cannot describe to you the sadness that descended over the health center. We felt as if we had lost a good friend. We had. He was the best chimp I have ever known.

When we performed a clinical examination, we were crushed by what we discovered. Charlie had died of a perforated ulcer. Things had been bothering him a lot more than he had been letting on. Not being able to keep his family at peace had taken a terrible toll on him.

One of the problems that a veterinarian encounters is the inability of his patients to tell him where it hurts so that they can be helped. If only Charlie could have let us know, we would have done anything to help him.

• • •

One of the advantages we have over the animal kingdom is that we can let someone know we need help. We can point to where it hurts. We can ask for help.

God's Word speaks to us directly about asking for what we need:

> Your Father knows what you need before you ask him (Matthew 6:8).
>
> Ask, and it will be given you; seek, and you will find; knock, and it will be opened to you. For every one who asks receives, and he who seeks finds, and to him who knocks it will be opened. Or what man of you, if his son asks him for bread, will give him a stone? Or if he asks for a fish, will give him a serpent? If you then, who are evil, know how to give good gifts to your children, how much more will your Father who is in heaven give good things to those who ask him! (Matthew 7:7-11).
>
> Whatever you ask in prayer, you will receive, if you have faith (Matthew 21:22).

Have you asked the Lord for anything lately? You may ask for help if you are in trouble. You may ask for forgiveness if you have sinned. You may ask for gifts, like love for others, patience, or wisdom. You may even ask for God to help a close friend. He commands us to ask. It is His nature to want to help us. That is what being a Father is all about.

CHAPTER THIRTY

So You Wanted to Play with a Lion

There is an oddity among zookeepers that I believe is unique to our profession: While on vacation we like to visit other zoos. Most people like to get away from what they normally do. But we like to interact with exotic animals and see the inner workings of other zoos. I did every time I got the chance.

One summer, while vacationing in Southern California, I took the opportunity to visit the small and immaculate zoo in San Jose. One of the exhibits that caught my interest was that of the large cats, which, of course, included lions. The zoo's director, Don Bracken, had departed radically from standard zoo philosophy by exhibiting only *tamed* cats. Ordinarily, zoos avoid taming wild animals because, as the old-timers had taught us, "It's the tame ones that get you!"—a saying that has been proven true throughout zoo histories. Incidents involving the death of zoo personnel have almost always been attributable to keepers trusting animals that were supposedly tame. We tend to forget that a wild animal, 14 to 21 times stronger than a man (which would be true of both lions and tigers), can have a bad day, regardless of whether it's tame or not.

Despite my knowing all this, I surprised myself by asking Don if I might be allowed to enter the African lion cage at his zoo. You see, the Los Angeles Zoo operated within the counsel of the wise. We had no tame lions with whom we might play. So I thought if I was ever going to have the experience of socializing with the king of beasts, this would probably be my only chance. The question popped out of my mouth before I had time to consider the consequences. What was more amazing than my question was the fact that Don, with a sly smile and a just-noticeable twinkle in his eye, said, "Sure, glad to oblige you."

With me was my wife Carol, our children, my wife's sister Darla, and her children. I sensed in Carol a certain wifely lack of enthusiasm for my adventure. Darla asked Carol if my going in with the lions bothered her. She answered yes. She thought that I was clearly showing a lack of wisdom and maturity by allowing myself to possibly be torn apart by lions in front of my children, wife, and relatives. She had a point. But I was an experience collector, and taking this experience back to my zoo would be a trophy too great to pass up.

Don and I made small talk as we walked to the cage together.

"The female is a sweetheart; you'll love her. She can't get enough attention," said Don as he fumbled for his keys.

"What about the male?" I probed.

"Moody."

"Moody?"

"Good days and bad days. You know how it is."

I didn't know how it was, but I nodded as if I did.

As we entered the cage, I kept my eye on the regal male, who was laying on the sleeping bench next to his mate. The bench stood about four feet off the ground. He stared at me, looking directly into my eyes for several seconds. His green eyes were alert but emotionless. At the same moment that he looked away, his ears went down and his tail began to twitch nervously He was in a mood.

"He's in a mood, isn't he, Don?"

"Believe so. Wouldn't be good to push him, I think."

"Push him?"

"Maybe it would be best just to leave him be."

"Should we step out?" I asked sincerely.

"The female's fine. We'll just spend a little time with her," he answered coolly.

"He doesn't mind if I pet the female, does he?"

"Never has before. We'll just keep an eye on him." (Why did I feel like I was playing "You Bet Your Life"?)

As I approached, the she-lion rolled over to be petted. Her 270-pound frame was about average size for a female. She looked at me lovingly, and I reached up and scratched her neck just behind the ear. She looked as if she were in ecstasy. She generated the lion equivalent of a purr, which, at about 50 times the intensity of a cat's purring, was a little disturbing. The male, who was just three feet away, glanced at me, turned away again, and growled. The growl, clearly distinguishable from the purr, raised my level of concern another notch. I looked back at Don, but he didn't seem concerned, so I stayed by the female's side, rubbed her stomach, and talked quietly to her.

"Rubbing her tummy makes her playful," Don warned. He was right. In a moment, she stood up on her bench and stretched. That stance revealed all of her usually concealed claws. They were long and quite capable of turning anything into shredded wheat. Then she yawned, exposing massive muscular jaws and long, deadly canines. She jumped off the bench and rubbed against my legs affectionately, whereupon I vigorously scratched her back. I was confronting death, showing off in front of family and relatives, and mentally recording an experience that most of my peers at the Los Angeles Zoo would never be able to duplicate. There was also a sense of mastery over a savage beast, the sense that this awesome predator was subjecting itself to a superior.

Boy, did all that change quickly!

The female walked about ten feet away from me and turned. She looked at me playfully, and then she bounced my way. She leaped up and grasped me around the chest. She squeezed tightly, forcing all the air from my lungs. My arms were pinned beneath her firm grip; I couldn't move them. I have never felt more helpless in my life. Her "play" strength was beyond my wildest imagination. As we stood there in a waltz position, it was obvious to me that she and I had two distinctly different desires. She wanted to play and I wanted to breathe. I turned to Don, who was smiling. He had that so-you-wanted-to-play-with-a-lion look (translation: "I told you so!").

"Don, she's playing a little rough," I said.

Literally, I felt as though I was in a vise, an immovable vise. I was beginning to panic; only pride kept me from losing my dignity. And, although the thought did occur to me, whimpering just didn't seem appropriate.

Don stepped forward and yelled, "Down, girl!" and hit her squarely on the head with the palm of his hand. He hit her hard, because the blow pulled me down a bit before she let go.

"Don't make her mad," I blurted out as I glanced at the male lion to see how he was feeling about the whole thing. His tail was twitching more than ever, and he was staring back and forth between Don and me. He didn't look like he would have taken that sort of blow from a mere human, and I was glad when Don said, "Hey, we have a tame jaguar named Christopher. Let me take you to his cage. He's a real sweetheart."

I left that lion cage a different man. For one thing, there was no more adrenaline in my adrenal glands. I was drained completely of energy. But more than that, I now had a realistic view of lions. Before the lioness hugged me, I saw lions as cartoons, fantasy playthings, the Hollywood image. In every old-time jungle movie ever made, the hero slays the ferocious lion, thus saving the life of his lady fair. The poor helpless lion, at the mercy of the hero's courage, strength, and stamina, never had a chance. Now I know for certain that those scenes were well choreographed. Lions are much more animal than I ever dreamed. Unless you have felt that kind of strength, I know it's difficult to imagine—just take my word for it.

At the same time, because of my up-close-and-personal experience, Scripture verses that included lions suddenly came alive for me. My newfound respect offered me a realistic perspective from which to view the writers' analogies. The first verses to come to mind for me were 1 Peter 5:8-9:

> Be sober, be watchful. Your adversary the devil prowls around like a roaring lion, seeking some one to devour. Resist him, firm in your faith, knowing that the same experience of suffering is required of your brotherhood throughout the world.

The phrase "a roaring lion" or the concept of lions roaring comes up here and some other places in Scripture, so it's important to know something about what a roar is or means so that we can learn what the Bible has to teach us.

A lion's roar may be heard over a distance of nearly five miles. The sound of the roar registers somewhere between 1 and 3 kHz. (The deepest bass gospel singer wouldn't be able to sing that loud without blowing every vocal cord in his larynx.) The roar is so loud and so low that, if you were standing next to the lion, you would feel the sound vibrate through your whole body.

So we know that a lion's roar is loud and powerful. But what does that have to do with Satan? Well, every reason for a lion to roar relates in some way to Satan's methodology.

For example, lions do most of their roaring at night under the cover of darkness. Darkness is where Satan does his work. Did you know that 3:00 in the morning is generally referred to as the "soul's midnight" because most people die in hospitals at about that time? Satan loves death, the pain it causes, and the faith it assaults. The majority of violent crimes, robberies, and rapes occur after the sun has fled the western sky. The Bible says it clearly: "Men loved darkness rather than light, because their deeds were evil" (John 3:19). Did you ever hear of a witches' coven or a satanic movement that called a meeting at twelve noon in an open field? Never. The occult meets at night. Do you remember the saying, "It's always darkest before the dawn"? Lions most often roar before the dawn, between 3:00 and 6:00 in the morning. That leads to the first and primary reason that lions roar:

Reason 1: Lions roar to create fear-paralyzing, heart-stopping, soul-wrenching, immobilizing fear. When they attack their prey, most of which is easily frightened anyway, they gain that much more of an advantage by roaring as they attack.

Satan's best tool is fear. Jesus knew that, and that's why He and the angels are forever saying, "Fear not." We are His sheep, and lions attack sheep. But the Lord is our Shepherd. And remember, "He who is in you is greater than he who is in the world" (1 John 4:4).

Let's consider some other reasons that lions roar:

Reason 2: Lions roar to gather their pride (their family). It is their way of saying, "Here I am."

Any speech delivered by the likes of Adolf Hitler, Fidel Castro, or Saddam Hussein is the evil lion saying, "Here I am." Any magazine stand selling pornography or any other woman-exploiting trash is Satan calling out, "Here I am."

Reason 3: Lions roar to herald their territory. The roar is hostile and says, "You will pay dearly if you try to take this territory away from me." An animal's territory is what it is most likely willing to die for. We can understand that, for some of us have given up fathers, brothers, and sons in battles to protect our country. We stand ready to do it again.

Satan, once he has claimed any territory, is savage about keeping it. He had claimed the Auca Indians in South America; they belonged to him. Jim Elliot was killed trying to claim the Aucas for the Lord Jesus. Did God not protect Jim? Yes and no. He offered Jim a crack at God's highest calling, and Jim took it. Then, as his reward, God took Jim through the gates of splendor. Satan won no victory over a man who demonstrated this highest calling. Jesus said, "Greater love has no man than this, that a man lay down his life for his friends" (John 15:13).

Reason 4: Lions use their roar to intimidate their competitors. They roar to run off other lions or leopards that might compete for prey.

That compares with Satan's attempts to convince us that someone is beyond our help—that he or she is too far gone. That's when Satan says that you'll get hurt if you become involved; you'll be arrested or sued if you try to help.

When we sense that Satan may be prowling around us, we must remember that God is always the stronger lion. We are not in a universe where a good lion and a bad lion are engaged in an eternal battle, where the tide swings this way and that and the outcome is uncertain. The great lion, the Lion of Judah (Revelation 5:5), King Jesus Himself, will prevail at the very moment He wishes to prevail—not a second too late or too soon. Satan is allowed to exist only to lose to the glory of God. Psalm 91 makes this clear:

He who dwells in the shelter of the most high,
    who abides in the shadow of the Almighty,
will say to the Lord, "My refuge and my fortress;
    my God, in whom I trust. . . .
Because you have made the Lord your refuge,
    the Most High your habitation,
No evil shall befall you,
    no scourge come near your tent.
For he will give his angels charge of you
    to guard you in all your ways.
On their hands they will bear you up,
    lest you dash your foot against stone.
You will tread on the lion and the adder,
    the young lion and the serpent you will
    trample under foot (verses 1-2, 9-13).

Yes, there are lions out there. But we travel with the greatest lion tamer of them all when we walk in faith with our Lord. When we do that, we see the lions at peace with all the animals they once preyed upon. And their roar will be heard no more.

Chapter Thirty-one

Just a Walk in the Park

The zoo security guard pulled his light-green Plymouth Valiant to an abrupt halt as he approached the aquatics section. There in the lengthening shadows of early evening was a large male chimpanzee walking slowly toward the back of the California sea lion exhibit. The guard had been at the zoo long enough to recognize that this was Toto, one of eight chimpanzees in the zoo. Of the eight, Toto was the worst possible chimp to be three-quarters of a mile from his cage. He was a former circus chimp, and in all likelihood he had been badly abused. By human standards, Toto was crazy, psychotic, and totally unpredictable. He could be gentle and friendly one moment and frenzied and violent the next.

The security guard rolled up his window and locked all the car doors. He reached for his walkie-talkie. He clicked it to the "on" position and it crackled to life. With his eyes fixed on the chimp that was now walking slowly toward his vehicle, he pressed the "send" button and whispered, "Sam, this is Joey . . . you there?"

He lifted the button and heard Sam reply, "Yeah, I'm here. What's up? Sounds like you're looking at a ghost . . . over."

"I wish I were. I'm in back of the chief keeper's shack just below the California sea lion exhibit, looking at Toto . . . over."

"Sounds like we have a problem. I'll notify the acting director and the capture team. Do your best to keep track of his whereabouts. Keep me posted. And Joey, be real careful. From what I've heard, Toto is bad news."

Joey kept track of Toto, and for whatever reason, Toto stayed near the chief's shack. He was, for all intents and purposes, lost. His zoo cage had been his territory for two years, and without help he would not be able to find his way back to it. Not knowing where he was, Toto was left with the problem of having nowhere to run. In his tangled mind he probably imagined he could be in enemy-occupied territory and was likely on the verge of emotional frenzy. He probably stayed in the area to be near the security guard who was keeping an eye on him.

Most of the capture team arrived at the same time and wisely stayed in their cars, waiting for Dr. Gale, the assistant director. Dr. Gale was an excellent animal-capture man worth waiting for, and the truth was that he would not have tolerated it any other way.

Toto was preoccupied with the sounds and smells of the immediate area and was satisfied that his company was staying in their cars. When Dr. Gale arrived, it was dark and only the horizon gave a hint that the sun had just set for the night. The zoo's dark green shrubbery nearly absorbed Toto's silhouette, and only his occasional movement betrayed his whereabouts. Dr. Gale directed the security guard to watch Toto, then motioned for the capture team to follow him out of the area. Once out of Toto's sight, they got out of their cars and listened to Dr. Gale's plan.

"We can't dart Toto with the capture gun; it is too dark to know if we hit him. He might fall into a pool, and worst of all, we may miss and scare him so that he leaves the zoo. Then he'd need to be shot before he hurt someone in the local neighborhood. If any of you have change, give it to me." They looked at each other, wondering what Dr. Gale had up his sleeve. But they knew him well enough not to question him. The change added up to a little less than two dollars. Dr. Gale sighed as he held it in his hand. He gave Bob Spellings 50 cents of it and told him to run and get a Coke from the nearest vending machine. He told the other men to drive up to the zoo's health center, open all the doors, and wait there for him and Toto. He told them he was going to attempt to walk Toto back to the cage; but he felt the fewer animal-care staff that Toto saw, the less chance there would be of Toto's flipping out and becoming violent.

Bob Spelling returned with the Coke and handed it to Dr. Gale, who took a sip and smiled a "wish-me-luck" smile. He waited for the men to clear the area, then walked slowly toward Toto. When he was nearing the chimp he could see that Toto was a bit apprehensive, and even in the dark he could see that Toto was beginning to stand; his hair was on end, and he looked as if he was about to charge.

Dr. Gale spoke softly, "You want something to drink, Toto?" Toto settled down and walked slowly forward and looked briefly at the cup and then into Dr. Gale's eyes. He reached for the man's hand and pulled it and the cup to his mouth and moaned contentedly. He poured most of the Coke into his mouth. Dr. Gale was beginning to wish the zoo served larger Cokes, because his plan was to lure Toto from vending machine to vending machine until they reached Toto's cage. But if Toto was going to finish everything so quickly, he might not follow to the next reward. Even worse, he might want more, and there would be no more to give him. It never took much to disturb Toto, and that was the last thing Dr. Gale wanted to have happen alone in the dark in the middle of the zoo. He was already questioning the wisdom of his own plan and looked around to see if any of the men were still nearby to suggest plan B. But he was alone. He wasn't really alone; there was a psychotic former circus chimp standing at his side drinking the last drop of Coke out of a cup that seemed smaller than ever.

Dr. Gale saw the chief keeper's building and concluded that he might be able to buy some time if he could lock Toto in the building. So he offered Toto his hand, and Toto took it—something he would have done as a young chimp but may not do for long as an old chimp who was six times as strong as the man who was leading him. Dr. Gale removed his keys from his pocket and unlocked the chief keeper's office. He walked into the dark office, hoping Toto would follow. He did. It was darker inside than out and Dr. Gale waited until he was sure Toto was fully inside.

Then Dr. Gale made a quick move and slipped out the door as quickly as he could. He slammed the door and locked it. His heart was pounding and beads of perspiration were forming on his forehead. He wiped it with his handkerchief and walked up to the window on his tiptoes to see if Toto was inside. He shaded his eyes from the glare of the streetlight that created reflections on the window and stared into the darkness of the office. He strained his eyes to see Toto, but could not locate the chimp. He felt a hand on his shoulder and slowly turned to find himself face to face with a disturbed Toto. In a mimicking fashion, Toto was also shielding his eyes from the reflection as he, too, stared into the darkness, trying to discover what had frightened the doctor out of the office.

"Let's go home, Toto," said the doctor, resigned to the first plan. Toto followed him to the next vending machine, where he purchased a small box of Good-and-Plenty candies. Toto enjoyed them immensely, but he would stop, sit down, and suck on them, so progress was somewhat impeded. Dr. Gale was now limited to one more purchase, and he was not even halfway to the health center. The wizened vet noticed a drinking fountain and turned the handle to show Toto that he could get a drink. Toto drank copious drafts of water and was captured by the novelty of the drinking device.

A lion roared from its night quarters. Toto stood straight up and rocked back and forth as if he were going to begin an aggressive display. He ran toward the lion and let out one loud scream as a warning to his unseen enemy. Then he looked back at Dr. Gale as if to say, "Well, I guess that takes care of that." Dr. Gale praised him in a soft voice and rewarded him with a Good-and-Plenty.

The Good-and-Plenty ran out, so Dr. Gale made the last purchase. A Payday candy bar slid out of the vending machine. Toto watched with interest as its wrapper was peeled away and a small piece was handed to him. Dr. Gale walked faster now, knowing he was on borrowed time. Toto grunted a "wait for me" sound and ran on all fours to catch up. The Payday was clearly a favorite choice. The chimp tugged at his benefactor's pant leg for another piece. Progress was now at a sufficient pace, and it looked as though they might make it to the health center after all.

As they rounded the corner at the mountain zebra exhibit, a terror-filled event took place. Ed Alonzo, the principal keeper, was waiting 50 yards away under the streetlight, monitoring the doctor's journey. If Dr. Gale got in trouble, Ed wanted to be there to help. But now Ed was in trouble. When Toto saw Ed under the streetlight, he stood up and hooted. He bolted away from Dr. Gale and ran at full speed toward the frozen principal keeper. Toto had injured others, and Ed fully expected to be bitten and beaten within an inch of his life, so he braced himself for the attack.

Toto looked menacing as he charged closer and closer. Ed swallowed and prepared himself for the awesome impact he was about to experience. At the last possible second, Toto pulled up short and stood up in front of Ed to greet him. Ed had been his keeper a few years before, and Toto was merely saying hello with a great deal of enthusiasm. Seeing a person that Toto remembered fondly had thoroughly piqued his interest. He had grown tired of the night's adventure, and Ed probably represented care and security. Toto reached for Ed's hand, which was shaking noticeably from the massive dose of adrenaline that had just been released into his system. The baton had been handed to Ed, so the last 100 yards were his to accomplish.

He and Toto walked up a narrow overgrown path, and when they reached the top, they could see the health center in full view. Toto released Ed's hand and again ran full speed until he had entered the health center's surgery door. He walked down the well-lighted hallway into the cage room and stood peering through the open door of his cage as if he were trying to make up his mind: "Shall I go in, or shall I stay out?" It was at this point that Bill Dickman, a brave and foolish keeper, ran full swing into Toto, bumping the chimp into his cage and slamming the door behind him. Toto hooted his displeasure, but he decided to be forgiving because he was so glad to be home.

• • •

This story reminds me that Jesus was willing to leave the safety of heaven to help me find my way back to Him. He cared about you and me so much that no risk was too great to ensure that we could come home. There was one difference in His story, however. He died to make it possible.

During our lives two things will always be true: 1) We will need to help others find the way to Jesus, remembering that someone else once helped us find the way. 2) We will need to help Christians who have taken a fork in the road and wandered off the path. When we see that happening in a Christian friend's life it would be good if we did not write him or her off as foolish or unworthy. It would be best if, like a shepherd, we left the 99 to rescue the one (*see* Luke 15:3-7). Isn't that what we would hope someone else would do for us?

After all, we really are our brother's keeper.

Chapter Thirty-two

Cherish the Butterflies

It's sad, but it's true. The earth is dying. It is wearing out. The Bible said it was going to, but until our generation I believe nobody took the following Bible passages seriously. But they are there and very plain to see if you have eyes to see. Let me show you.

Psalm 102:26 tells us that the earth will "wear out like a garment." Revelation 11:18 warns that the time will come "for destroying the destroyers of the earth." Isaiah the prophet had the clearest vision of what would happen, and he even knew who would cause it. The scene is earth and the final demise of Satan. There are people standing around the edge of a great pit. They are looking at Satan and saying, "Is this the man who made the earth tremble, who shook kingdoms, who made the world like a desert?" Like a desert—barren, lacking fresh water, and devoid of abundant life. Does it seem possible that our world, whose land mass is 75 percent forest, could become a desert? Fifty years ago that scripture would have been offered as a symbolic overstatement. But not anymore.

Isaiah further amplifies in 10:19, "The remnant of the trees of his forest will be so few that a child can write them down." What kind of numbers can a child conceive? Ten, maybe 20. When Satan is cast into the pit the trees have something to say. "The cypresses rejoice at you, the cedars of Lebanon, saying, 'Since you were laid low, no hewer [woodcutter] comes up against us'" (Isaiah 14:18).

Let us consider the history of Israel. G. S. Cansdale, in his wonderful book *All the Animals of Bible Lands,* states, "Man has left his mark all over the world, but the lands of the Bible have been occupied and used since the birth of civilization, so it is not surprising that he has done more damage there than almost anywhere else, leaving great areas of soil impoverished or even eroded down to bare rock. This is reflected in the flora, poor in species and poor on the ground and this in turn in the fauna." When Abraham came to the Promised Land it was a woodland. His only source of fuel was wood, so he and those after him began to cut down the trees and clear the land. Because of wars the land was often salted so that nothing would grow for long periods of time. It began as a land flowing with milk and honey but it became an ecological nightmare.

Satan has been busy throughout history at the task of destroying the earth, but it seems to have become a higher priority in our age of technology. All the world is following the pattern of Israel. In Southern California one out of eight trees is dying because of air pollution. But the western United States is better off than the eastern side. The auto and steel industries are belching millions of tons of sulphur dioxide into the atmosphere. Rain clouds pick it up and redistribute it all over the East Coast and Canada. Oak trees are dying by the thousands, and whole forests are being stunted. Fish are becoming unable to reproduce because of metal build-ups caused by the acid rains. Robert H. Boyle writes in his sobering book, *Acid Rain,* that we are absolutely devastating Canada with our toxic emissions. The effects of acid rain originating in the eastern United States to date include killing all the fish in 1,200 lakes. There are 3,400 other lakes that are nearly dead; 11,400 are at risk; and in another 20 years 48,500 lakes are likely to lose their fish.

Germany is even further down the road. One out of three trees in their famous Black Forest is dying because of smog damage. Pollution is not the only problem that trees are experiencing worldwide. Direct cutting in South America is taking one acre of forest every 1.2 seconds—that's 50 acres per minute, or 42,000 square miles a year. These facts were gleaned from Paul and Anne Ehrlich's powerful book, *Extinction.*

Did you know that more than three million acres of ground are paved over every year? Isaiah 5:8 says, "Woe to those who join house to house, who add field to field, until there is no more room." Satan's desert may not be as far into the future as we would like to believe. He is not in "the pit" yet, and he is actively working at the destruction of the earth.

What does Satan get out of all this? A chance to kill many people. The world's trees filter pollution out of the air and they exchange carbon dioxide for oxygen. They also liberate millions of gallons of water into the atmosphere. The water becomes rain. We need those trees. Satan knows all this, but he is now and has always been a murderer. What an effective way of killing millions. Africa is already experiencing the beginning of the ecological end. The famines in that country are the result of poor land management and a total disregard for ecological balance.

Isaiah saw it all. "The earth mourns and withers. . . . The earth lies polluted under its inhabitants. . . . The earth is utterly broken, the earth is rent asunder, the earth is violently shaken" (24:4-5, 19). Isaiah was given a look at what the future of the earth would include. As he wrote, he was accounting for events that would not occur for 2,700 years. He saw our world as it is today, and it's happening just as he said it would. He saw the effects; we know the causes. Decimation of species, chemical pollution, destruction of habitat, and overuse—these are the weapons we have used to destroy the earth.

How do you think God feels about the way we are treating His magnificent creation? Not good, I think. Dante said, "Nature is the art of God." We are defacing His art. His art is functional art. It takes care of us.

Think about John Drinkwater's poetry:

> When you defile the pleasant streams,
> And the wild birds' abiding place.
> You massacre a million dreams,
> And cast your spittle in God's face.

Why is God putting up with our meaningless and futile defacement of His priceless work of art? I believe there is a complete explanation in Romans 8:19-20:

> The creation waits with eager longing for the revealing of the sons of God; for the creation was subjected to futility, not of its own will but by the will of him who subjected it in hope.

Let me paraphrase the above verses. I think you will be moved by what God's spirit has revealed through the apostle Paul: All of nature is awaiting, with enthusiasm and deep longing, for everyone who is going to come to the Lord to do so. God has ordered nature to put up with man's needless abuse. Nature didn't want to, but God ordered nature to take man's abuse so that man could have more time to come to Him. If you want to get a concrete picture of what this verse is saying, consider this illustration.

Michelangelo is in his studio. Around the room are several of his most cherished masterpieces. His love and greatest skills are evident in every stroke of the brush and cut of the chisel. His work praises his genius and expresses his deepest thoughts. Suddenly, a servant boy that he loves dearly throws open the studio door. It is evident that he is severely mentally disturbed. He doesn't comprehend the love of the master artist and is, in fact, needlessly jealous of his abilities and authority. The servant boy rushes forward and slashes many of the paintings and dashes many of the sculptures to the floor. Much of the art is beyond repair and lost forever. Michelangelo walks to the servant boy and holds him in a long embrace. He then speaks softly, "My boy, you mean more to me than the art. I want you to be my son. We can work this out." Michelangelo shares with the other servants that for now the boy is not to be punished. The boy will be given more time to be willing for adoption. The servants express their anger and shock at what has happened but they promise to stand with the master's choice.

Our Father never misses a sparrow's fall. The fact that He has not destroyed us for what we have done to His beautiful creation is all the assurance we should ever need of His love.

May I give you more of an idea of what it means for the creation to have been subjected to futility? We need only to look at what has happened to our own country to get an idea of the needless pain that nature has suffered on our behalf.

When our forefathers set foot on this continent they found that it was teeming with life. There were turkeys to be shot so that the early colonists could make it through that first severe winter. There were hooved animals on every hillside and in every valley. Fish were plentiful in every sparkling stream. One animal dominated the scene and provided meat and hide in generous abundance. That was the American bison. When the pilgrims stepped onto Plymouth Rock, it is estimated that North America sustained a population of 75 million of the impressive hooved Goliaths.

The North American Indians killed only what they needed. And throughout the 1700s there were not enough settlers to pose a threat to the bisons' existence.

All this wonderful balance began to erode by 1810. A European market developed for meat and hides, and buffalo hunting began in earnest. Names like Buffalo Bill Cody, Kit Carson, and Jim Bridger became household words. They were the great white hunters of our continent and their time. By 1832 the last buffalo east of the Mississippi was killed. David A. Dary says all this in his great book *The Buffalo Book: The Saga of an American Symbol.*

Hunting became a sport and people were encouraged to shoot the buffalo from trains as they journeyed westward. No thought was given to whether they might be wasting a valuable resource or whether they just wounded or actually killed the beasts they shot from the moving trains.

When United States government officials realized how dependent the Indians were on the bison, they encouraged eradication of the species. The Indians could be relegated to reservations more easily if they were starving and cold.

By 1895 there were less than 400 buffalo in existence. We killed almost the total population of 75 million in a mere 85 years.

There were other casualties of the westward movement. As we settled the West we killed the wolves, both the red and grey. There are about 1,600 left in the wild. There used to be more than a million.

The largest bird in North America, the condor, suffered an indirect slaughter. They were carrion eaters, and we had wasted their food supply. God had designed them to eat dead animals, especially dead bison. They were His cleanup crew. But so much of their food had been eradicated that they began to starve to death. When America was first set tled, there were close to 1.5 million condors. But as recently as 1967 there were only 26 California condors. Because of the captive breeding program, we have slowly brought the population back to just less than 100.

Our American symbol, the bald eagle, has not fared too well, either. We have less than one-tenth of the original population. Insecticides and destruction of habitat took them.

Think about the demise of the great whales. Farley Mowat, in his moving account, *A Whale for the Killing,* shows the decline of the whale population between the years of 1930 and 1972. Some species that had numbered in the hundreds of thousands have dropped 75, 80, even 90 percent of their total population. The grey whale is extinct altogether, and the right whale and blue whale are on the brink of extinction.

Whales are fantastic animals. They have I.Q.s that rival man's. They cooperate with each other when they hunt, they care for each other when they get sick, and they sing songs that can be heard by other whales more than 30 miles away. They have been quietly tolerant of man's abuse to their species. They have remained subject to the futility of man as God had decreed.

And they have suffered. The statistics reveal the decline of the whales, but they do not demonstrate the agony they have endured. The principal method of killing whales has always been harpooning. The sensitive animals were repeatedly harpooned and forced to drag boats for miles as they tried to keep up with their family groups. When they became too exhausted to swim any longer, the whalers would spear them over and over until loss of blood slowly but surely claimed their lives. This is a warm-blooded animal that nurses its young and loves its family.

One of the most sickening facts to surface in recent years involves the United States Navy. Farley Mowat records this in *A Whale for the Killing:*

> Until after the Second World War there were almost no sightings of great whales off the south of Newfoundland. Then, in the late 1940s, U.S. Naval aircraft flying out of the leased base at Argentina in southwest Newfoundland began spotting an

> occasional big whale. News of these sightings came to light in the mid-1950s when it was learned that whales had become a useful addition to the Navy's antisubmarine training. Aircraft crews, engaged in practice patrol work, had been instructed to pretend that any whales they spotted were Russian submarines. The whales became targets for cannon fire, rockets, bombs, and depth charges!

In 1957 an outcry by Harold Horwood, a crusading columnist on the *St. John's Evening Telegram,* resulted in a promise from the Argentina officials that whales would no longer be used as targets.

The number of whales either killed, wounded, or attacked by the Navy over a ten-year period was never released. Presumably, it was classified information.

I could go on and on until you became overloaded with facts, statistics, and stories of man's inhumanity to the animal kingdom. I could tell you that there are less than 250 grizzly bears left in the United States. I could tell you that until they became protected, the mountain lion was hunted almost to extinction. If I were to include worldwide statistics, you would discover that in your lifetime you may expect to hear about the extinction of the following animals: mountain gorillas, cheetahs, African elephants, rhinos, and thousands of other lesser-known species.

At the present rate of extinction, we will be losing one-fifth of the world's species by the end of this century. There are times that I wish the animals would fight back. They could, you know. There are enough bees or bacteria to kill every man, woman, and child on the earth. But they won't, because they have been subjected.

There may be no greater example of God's patience with man than His putting up with man's abuse of His great creation. Remember that this is all to give time for people to come to the Lord Jesus Christ.

I agree with André Crouch: "I don't know why Jesus loves me but I'm glad, so glad He did." Our proper response to His great love is to share it. We should be bringing people to Jesus.

I've told you the bad news. Now let me tell you the good news: this earth will pass away, as will the present heaven, and the Lord will make new ones. They will be far better creations and they will be populated with perfect, sinless, and forgiven people. He will set His children on a cloud somewhere in eternity and speak these new creations into existence. You and I may be there to see it. The Scripture says that the new earth will have neither sun nor moon, for it will be illuminated by the glory of the Lord Himself. The seas will be no more, but no one will be disappointed. This just means that there will be lakefront property for everyone. Lots of eagles, I bet, filling crystal-clear skies. Did I tell you about the animals? They will all be tame. If you want to hug a lion, no problem. If you want to pick up a cobra, go ahead. Consider these verses from the book of Isaiah:

> The wolf shall dwell with the lamb,
> and the leopard shall lie down with the kid,
> and the calf and the lion and the fatling together,
> and a little child shall lead them.
> The cow and the bear shall feed;
> their young shall lie down together;
> and the lion shall eat straw like the ox.
> The suckling child shall play over the hole of the asp,
> and the weaned child shall put his hand on the adder's den.
> They shall not hurt or destroy
> in all my holy mountain;
> for the earth shall be full of the knowledge of the Lord as the waters cover the sea (Isaiah 11:6-9).

If you think that sounds great, then enjoy what the apostle Paul shares with us in 1 Corinthians 2:9:

> No eye has seen, nor ear heard, nor the heart of man conceived, what God has prepared for those who love him.

We only see a small band of the colors that exist in the universe—just those of the rainbow. They are beautiful, but we haven't seen anything yet. Moths see a whole spectrum of colors we have never seen, but will.

We hear in a small band of the sounds that exist. Foxes hear a far wider range than we do. We are thrilled to hear orchestras and choirs play in eight octaves, but just wait for the thrill of hearing angel choirs burst forth in 80 octaves. Our music will sound so incomplete.

Go ahead. Push the limits of your imagination. Try and picture wonders far beyond any you have ever known. Well, God is planning things immeasurably better than you have just imagined. Don't you love God for that? If you don't, won't you try? You just won't want to miss out on the future that He has planned for those who love Him.